Turnstones 1

An English course for Scotland

Anne Donovan

Brian Fitzpatrick

Sheila Hughes

Liz Niven

Jenny Allan

Robbie Robertson (editor)

Hodder & Stoughton

A MEMBER OF THE HODDER HEADLINE GROUP

Copyright text
p7 *Stone Cold* © Robert Swindells, Puffin Books; p33, 44 From *The Spark Gap* © Julie Bertagna.
First published in 1996 by Mammoth, an imprint of Egmont Children's Books Limited and used with
permission; p47 *Maura's Angel* by Lynne Reid Banks, Nelson Thornes Ltd; p59 '*November Night, Edinburgh*'
from *COLLECTED POEMS* by Norman MacCaig published by Hogarth Press. Used by permission of The
Random House Group Limited; p61 *The Tattie Bogle* by Lavinia Derwent, permission granted by Mary Baxter;
p68 *David's Story* © Anne Donovan; p81 *Wigtown Ploughman* by John McNellie; p97 *Space Invaders* by
Alan Spence, Hodder & Stoughton; p137, 138 Derewianka B *Exploring How Texts Work*, Primary English
Teaching Association, Sydney; p140 *A Book of One's Own* by Paul Johnson, Hodder & Stoughton

Copyright photographs
Bill Varie/CORBIS 108; C M Dixon Photo Resources 37; Joan Eardley 86, 87, 88; Frank Lane Picture Agency
4; Irn Bru 104; Life File 7, 11; National Museums of Scotland 80; Popperfoto 21;

*Every effort has been made to trace copyright holders of material produced in this book. Any rights not acknowledged
here will be acknowledged in subsequent printings if notice is given to the publisher.*

Orders: please contact Bookpoint Ltd, 130 Milton Park, Abingdon, Oxon OX14 4SB.
Telephone: (44) 01235 827720. Fax: (44) 01235 400454. Lines are open from 9.00 - 6.00, Monday to
Saturday, with a 24 hour message answering service. Email address: orders@bookpoint.co.uk

British Library Cataloguing in Publication Data
A catalogue record for this title is available from the British Library

ISBN 0 340 79036 9

Published by Hodder & Stoughton Educational Scotland
First Published 2001
Impression number   10 9 8 7 6 5 4 3
Year   2007 2006 2005 2004 2003 2002

Copyright © 2001 Anne Donovan, Brian Fitzpatrick, Sheila Hughes, Liz Niven, Jenny Allan, Robbie Robertson

Cover photo from David Rudkin
Designed and typeset by Mind's Eye Design, Lewes
Printed in Italy for Hodder & Stoughton Educational, a division of Hodder Headline Plc,
338 Euston Road, London NW1 3BH.

Contents

About Turnstones 1

As you read, stop and note questions in your jotter. Your teacher or a partner will help with answers.

What's a turnstone?

A turnstone is a bird about 25cm long found on seacoasts around the world. You can see it on the Scottish seashore especially in winter, but the bird is found across Western Europe, America and the rest of the world. We think **Turnstones 1** is something like this bird and that's why we've given the book its name.

Resources

You can find out more about the bird called the turnstone at
www.wildfowl.nildram.co.uk/turnstone.htm

Why *Turnstones 1* ?

There are two reasons:

1. The turnstone makes its living turning over stones and seaweed to find its food. **Turnstones 1** is to help you learn how language works. The stones you turn when you're doing this are bits of writing, speech, pictures, music, and so on. The turning over involves reading, talking, listening and watching - and writing.

2. The turnstone is also a world traveller. **Turnstones 1** is a book intended for Scottish schools and in it you'll find Scotland well represented, especially in terms of its main languages, English and Scots. But you'll also be asked to step outside Scotland.   From time to time there will be things from around the world; this is the bigger world where the turnstones fly.

Using Turnstones 1

English has a central place in your school studies. If you can't use and understand the English language to the best of your ability by the time you leave school you might as well never leave your own place, never switch on a TV or radio, never read a paper, and never turn to a computer game for relaxation.

Turnstones 1 will ask you to begin learning about all the language skills - reading, talking, listening and watching - and in particular the skill of writing.

We don't expect you to use ***Turnstones 1*** from the beginning working through to the end. But you should not start jumping about in it **until you've read, completed and understood the first two sections**.

In the margin of a lot of pages you'll find icons - special marks with particular meanings. Below you will find a list of these icons with the explanations of what they mean.

You'll also see from time to time that a word has been printed in different colours. This tells you that the meaning of the word can be found perhaps in a panel in the margin, certainly in the Glossary on pages 141 to 144. Like a **dictionary** the Glossary is alphabetically arranged.

Sometimes you will work with the whole team: your teacher, the rest of the class. Sometimes you will work with a smaller team of 3, 4, 5 or 6 other pupils. Sometimes you will work with one special partner and sometimes you will be on your own but you'll always have support round about you. Don't forget to use it.

Glossary

Dictionary
A book listing words in alphabetical order, giving their meanings, how they are said and sometimes their histories.

ICONS	MEANINGS
STOP!	Stop reading at this point and start doing something else. We'll tell you what.
pages 0-0	Later parts of **Turnstones 1** at page(s) such-and-such can be connected to this section or part of a section.
pages 0-0	Earlier parts of **Turnstones 1** at page(s) such-and-such can be connected to this section or part of a section.
	There is something on the CD-ROM which can be connected to this section or part of a section.

Turnstones 1 is a book **and** a CD-ROM. The book has print, drawings, and pictures. The CD-ROM has these too but it also has sound. The CD-ROM gives lots more information and when you see the CD icon you should think of switching to the CD if you want to find *activities* similar to those you are doing or have done and/or texts related to those you have just read.

We hope you will enjoy using Turnstones.

Anne Donovan

Brian Fitzpatrick

Sheila Hughes

Liz Niven

Jenny Allan

Robbie Robertson (Editor)

1 Meeting the challenge part one

Reading about personal feelings

Most challenges are solved in stages and most challenges have more than one solution! You can use questions to help you read a text. We will describe the questions and stages you'll need to go through to help you find your own answers.

Glossary

Text
Any made thing which conveys information, e.g. writing, picture, recorded conversation, sound, etc.

Stage One

You'll need to work with a partner. **Read** the following extract from a novel (or maybe your teacher will read it out for the whole class). As you are reading or listening **try to think** exactly what this extract is about.

Your only **clue** is that the boy is living rough in the streets of London.

This text is available for DARTs techniques

The last days of January were a swine. I nearly went back to Vince. I mean it. It snowed every day so the pavements were thick with slush, and nothing gets inside a pair of trainers like slush can. Ginger and I lurked in subways and doorways as much as we could but our feet were constantly wet and freezing just the same. Night after night, frost turned the slush to grey iron and crept into our damp bedding to stiffen footwear and make sleep impossible. And if you think it's bound to make the punters more generous with their change, seeing kids wet and shivering, forget it. It had the opposite effect. Everybody slogged grimly by and their hands never left their pockets unless they were wearing gloves. Nobody stopped. Maybe they thought they'd die if they stopped, like explorers at the South Pole.

We grew hungry. Really hungry. The cold seems to settle in your bones when there's nothing in your stomach. You can't shift it. We tried everything – stamping our feet, running on the spot, blowing into our hands, huddling together in the subway. It was no use. All we could do was keep moving through sleepless nights and days that merged into one another till we no longer knew what day it was or whether it was morning or evening... Once we'd been turned away from a hostel, we'd make our way to one of the stations – King's Cross or St Pancras, mostly – to wait for the Sally Army. The walk would keep us from hypothermia, and the Sally Army came round about midnight with soup or sandwiches. It was free grub so there was always a mob, but we usually scored a butty apiece or a mug of soup, and that's what kept us alive till February came, and the thaw.

Oh, by the way, if you're wondering why I wasn't attending job interviews all this time, I can enlighten you. My clothes were sodden rags. My fingernails were long black claws, I had matted hair down to my shoulders and I stank. I wanted work all right – would have killed for it – but I knew I hadn't a hope of being taken on in that condition. I wouldn't have hired me.

From Stone Cold by Robert Swindells (Puffin, 1995).

With your partner **talk** about what is going on in this part of the novel. **Think up** five questions about the novel for another pair to answer. The questions should help the others to work out what is going on for themselves. For example, a question might be, *What time of year is it?* This is a fact, and the other pair won't have to work very hard to come up with the answer: *winter*, or *January*.

But a questions like, *What was the weather like?* or *How did the weather affect the people in the story?* are more difficult. Questions like this mean that they'll have to read the passage really carefully to find the answers.

When you have worked out some questions to ask, swopped them and answered the questions of the other pair, meet together and **exchange** your answers. How well did you do? How well did they do? Try to agree which pair did best. Try to work out why one group did better than the others.

Stage one should not be too difficult. But remember this is only your first task. When you've finished this stage another awaits you…

 Look at the icon in the margin: this tells you to stop reading and to do something else!

Stage two

Keep working with your partner. Now that you have worked out what the passage is about, think very carefully about how you feel about the boy in the story. Here is a way to do this.

Draw two columns in your jotter. Head one **Feelings** and the other **Reasons**. Remember that the author has a very clear idea of how *he wants you* to feel about his character and has used words in particular ways to put *his* ideas into *your* head. See if you can spot the clues he gives you. We've given you two examples to start you off.

Wouldn't you be sad if you were in such a situation? Be prepared to share your ideas with the rest of the class later.

Feelings	Reasons
sad	*nothing gets in trainers like slush can*
cold, miserable	*frost…crept into our damp bedding*
?	?

> Please don't do this on the book (your teacher won't be happy and we'll get into trouble!) but if you have a **copy** of the passage you could *highlight* or *underline* the words and phrases that make you feel a certain way about the boy. This would speed up the task enormously, wouldn't it?

Done that? Well, you've solved your first reading problem! Move on!

Stage three

Now for the big **free offer**. We are going to give you some **keys**. The keys are really important questions that you should ask *any* text you are reading, watching or listening to. Asking these questions will help you to work out what is going on.

Keep these keys safe. Maybe even **write them down**. You'll certainly need them in the future. You will also discover more as you move through *Turnstones 1*.

Some keys for getting to grips with reading texts

Questions to ask a text

1 **What** are you about? *Is it obvious? Is anything being hidden? How do I know?*

2 **Who made you?** *Is the author really present? Or hidden? Or is the author pretending to be someone else? Which?* **Who** *is the author?*

3 **Who are you made for?** *What is the* target audience*? Me? Or someone else? Who?*

4 **How were you made?** *Has the author used words, pictures or sounds in a particular way? How do they make me feel or think?*

5 **Why were you made?** *Is it, maybe, intended to make me feel in a certain way, to think in a certain way, or is it trying to persuade me to do something?*

6 **When were you made?** *In my time? A long time ago? When? How do I know?*

Glossary

Target audience
The particular audience at which a text is being aimed.

The reading challenge

See Visual Workpoints V5 and V20 for interesting texts.

In a group, or with a partner, **choose a text**, any text, and ask it the key questions. The text could be a poem, a picture, or a cornflakes packet – whatever you like. **Discuss** your answers before writing them down. Do you agree, or disagree? If you disagree explore your differences.

2 Meeting the challenge part two

Writing about personal feelings

Reading involves spotting clues and solving problems. **Writing** means you have to *set clues* for your reader and *give them problems* to solve. To do this we are going to ask you to meet certain challenges.

Challenge

Hint: you have to work through **stages**.

We are about to ask you to write something. You will have to make some **decisions** about this writing task before you begin. How are you going to do it?

STOP!
What do you think these stages might be? **Talk** about this with a partner. Don't read any more. Start talking.

Done that? **Compare** *your* solutions with others in the class.

pages 7-10

What you've probably worked out is that there are keys, just as with reading, which will help you with the writing challenges.

Writing keys are similar to reading keys, almost like mirrors of them, but there are some differences.

Knowing about the keys is not enough. *You are in command*. You have to think carefully how to make them *work*. Which locks will the keys open? We can't tell you. Nobody can. It's up to you.

Here are the keys that will help you meet your *writing* challenges. Note them down. Talk about them with a partner. *Remember them!*

Some keys for getting to grips with writing

Questions to ask yourself

1 **Who are you?** *As the writer, are you yourself or are you pretending to be someone else? What kind of person are you?*

2 **Who are you writing for?** *What is your target audience? Someone your own age? Someone else? Who?*

3 **What are you trying to do with your writing?** *Entertain your reader? Make them laugh? Make them feel sad? Tell them how to do something? Persuade them to buy something? Make them think?*

4 **What is going to happen in your writing?** *What are the stages? These might be events, things that are going to happen in a story, or they might be steps to follow in a set of instructions. How many stages are there? How are they joined together? Where do they begin? Where will they end?*

5 **Where is it going to take place?** *If you're writing fiction think about place, time of day, weather, and so on. If you're writing non-fiction think about the pattern of what you are going to write.*

6 **How are you going to write it?** *What words will you choose? What kind of sentences will you use? If you're writing fiction, will you use lots of dialogue, or will it be more descriptive?*

Glossary

Fiction
A form of invented story sometimes based on real events and characters but usually imaginary.

Non-fiction
A text, usually written, dealing with facts, real people and events which actually happened.

Dialogue
The words used by characters, usually in scripts and fiction, *and* a conversation between people.

---

pages 7-8

With a partner **look again** at the extract from the novel by Robert Swindells. **Imagine** *you* are the author. How could you have used the writing keys to help you write the extract?

page 14

We've given you some answers at the end of this section of **_Turnstones 1_** but work out *your* answers before going to it. After you've checked your answers, come back to this page to take up the writing challenge.

The writing challenge

- **Imagine** you are the boy in the extract from the novel by Robert Swindells. *You have run away from home because you were being beaten up by your mum's husband. You can't bring yourself to think of him as your dad because your dad's dead.*

- **Write a letter** to your sister letting her know how miserable you are, but telling her that *you* will be alright.

- Your **challenge** is to include lots of thoughts and feelings but not much action.

Work with your partner sorting out some ideas using the keys and then write your letter by yourself.

Once you've finished it, exchange your story with your partner. How well do you think your stories have met the challenge? To judge your stories ask yourselves these questions:

- Are they *easy to read* and understand?

- What *interesting ideas* do they have?

- Do they have *thoughts* you can *understand*, and *feelings* you can *feel*?

- Have you used the *best words* you can think of?

Talk about your stories. How else could they be improved? Maybe your teacher will advise.

By reading the extract from *Stone Cold* and writing your letter, you have been covering one of the main purposes of reading and writing: to explore **personal feelings**.

LOOKING AT THE EXTRACT

Some answers

 1 *I'm a teenage boy who has run away from home.*

 2 *I'm writing for teenagers about the problems I faced – which they should be aware of.*

 3 *I want my reader to know what I'm thinking and how miserable I feel.*

 4 *Not many different events because I want you to concentrate on how I feel.*

 5 *London doorway. Winter. Cold atmosphere.*

 6 *I need lots of cold, miserable descriptive words. I will use short sentences when I'm angry and long sentences to show I'm puzzled and confused.*

How well did your answers match ours?

Remember: most problems to do with language have more than one solution. Your solution may be different from ours. This does not mean that we are right and you are wrong. If you can produce *good reasons* for what you say, *you are almost certainly right*.

So, if *your* answers are different from what *we* said when we used the writing keys, can you give *good* reasons for your decisions? Talk about this in class.

3 Writing about yourself part one

How to start

> Writing about yourself may sound simple but it isn't always easy to do. There are many different approaches to **autobiographical writing** so now we're going to ask you to think about – and practise – a few ways of doing it.

Every human life is a story

Making choices

First, you need to **choose** which parts of your life you're going to write about. An account of every detail of your life would, almost certainly, be quite boring! Ours would be. And could you remember it all? We couldn't. So how do you choose which bits to write about?

A deeply memorable experience?

Sometimes it's obvious. If you can remember an *experience* in detail it is, most likely, because it was very important to you. Such experiences can also be good starting points for writing. Here are some examples:

- going into hospital

- a special birthday

- moving house or school

- getting (or losing) a pet.

Read the following extract to *understand* what we mean.

The thing that sticks in my mind most from when I was very young is the first time I stole something; I was about two years old at the time. My mother and I were visiting friends who had some older children who had practically every toy under the sun because they had rich relatives who spoilt them. Anyway, even at such an early age I wondered why they could have so many lovely toys when all I had was a few cars, a teddy bear and an old, bedraggled doll. So I decided I would have some of their toys. I remember picking out the things that would not be missed and stuffing them behind the pillow in my pram which was very easy to climb into. When it was time to go home I started taking the toys out. My mum was very angry and brought me back with the toys. I had to say sorry and I remember feeling very resentful because I thought it just was not fair – they had everything I wanted and I didn't.

From 'Me and My History' by Anna Leitrim in **Our Lives, Young People's Autobiographies** (ILEA English Centre, 1979)

Anna Leitrim is writing about a very simple incident from her childhood. What makes it important is the way she tells us her **thoughts** and **feelings** about the incident, as well as giving us the **facts**. She felt it was very unfair that these children had so many things she wanted. She is very **honest** about these feelings and we can see why she remembers the incident so well.

Writing about it

Write a **paragraph** about an incident you remember from *your* childhood, saying what you thought and felt, as well as giving the facts. Be honest. Exchange your paragraph for a partner's. Talk together about how well the experiences have been told, and why they have stayed with you both.

Think about what's important

Sometimes we need to take some time to think about the important events in our lives. One way of doing this is to make a **time line** or map of life so far.

Making a time line

Draw a line to represent *your* life. (It doesn't *need* to be a straight line: you can make it wavy, spiral, zig-zag, anything you like.) *But be sure to leave enough space round it for drawing.* Make marks on your line to represent each year of your life (if you need to) and number them. Think back over your life and make a mark like an asterisk (*) to represent all the things that have happened to you and that you remember as being important. Don't write your experiences down. Just remember them, putting an asterisk against each year when something important happened. You don't have to have one asterisk for every year and you can have as many asterisks as you like. Here's an example of a time line. It doesn't use year marks because the years are obvious.

Once you've done your line, **share** it with a partner. Tell them what each asterisk represents and why the event is important to *you*. Talking to them will help you to decide which event in your life to write about.

Writing it down

Pick *one event* and **write** about it in more detail (three or four paragraphs will be enough.) Or, if you prefer, you could take a few events which are linked in some way (for example, if you had an illness on several occasions over several years) and write about them together.

Then go deeper – explore your feelings, to find out who you really are...

The importance of names

For most of us, our **names** are very important. Parents take a lot of care choosing names for their children and most people have strong feelings about names. Some people like their name and feel it suits them. They're happy but others are not! Some people prefer to use a nickname or a different name to the one they were given – *Curly* rather than *Archibald*, *May* rather than *Amy*. Some people get a new name, maybe in childhood, and it sticks. Names and autobiographies? You could write books about them (and many have)! You can find some books and **web**sites on the subject in Resources.

Changing self – changing names

The people of the Lakota tribe in America traditionally have several names throughout their lives. They get **new names** at important points in their lives. Therefore their names reflect directly the events of their life. For example the first given names may express appearance or your place in the family:

> **Padai** *(twin)*
> **Hakadeh** *(given to a boy who was last in his family)*
> **Pretty Shield** *(after her grandfather's war shield)*

Later names may be associated with important places:

> **Tsoai-talee** *(Rock-Tree boy)*
> **Hutuxt** *(Star)*

Names may suggest achievements or skills:

> **Okuhhatuh** *(making medicine)*
> **Ohiyeas** *(winner – named after winning a lacrosse game)*
> **Aleek-chea-ahoosh** or **Plenty-coups** *(to count coups was to touch a live enemy and get away without being harmed, so this name suggests a lot of success in battles)*

Names (of animals or weather) can reflect your character. Forceful characters were given names of animals like *Buffalo* or *Bear* while more peaceful ones were called *Swift Bird* or *Blue Sky*.

From 'Plains Indian Names' by Hertha D. Wong in **Autobiography and Postmodernism** (University of Massachusetts Press, 1994).

Thinking

Take a few minutes to **reflect** on (think about) all the things that names can suggest about people. (You may want to discuss this with a partner, or a group, or with your teacher.) Then, **make a note** of *your* answers to the following questions.

1 What is my full name?

2 Do I know why I was given my forename? Does my name have a meaning? Was I, for example, called after a relative?

3 Do I like my name? Why, or why not?

4 Are there variations of my name I don't like? Why, or why not?

5 Do I have a nickname? Who calls me by it and what does it mean? Do I like it?

 6 If I could pick my own name, what name(s) would I choose?

Writing it down

Now **write** a few paragraphs reflecting on – thinking about – *your name* and *your feelings* about it.

Look back over your time line. Were there any important points in your life when you might have received a new name – if you'd been a native American? What were they? If you can, write (or draw) the name(s) you think you might have received at these times in your life. Talk with a partner.

4 Writing about yourself part two

Family and self

> Our families can be important in shaping who we are and how we feel about ourselves. Looking at where our families have come from and how that affects our lives can be another way of starting to think about autobiography.

Here are some examples of autobiographical writing which explore the idea of the writer's family background. The first two are from an anthology of Scottish writers whose families originally came from Ireland.

Ireland. As far back as I can remember, the name was always around, in the air. ...As a child in fifties Glasgow, it was always around like a relative you'd never met but knew you'd like when you did. Always around in the letters that would come, 'Oh, it's from Peggy in Wexford' or, 'Mary in Bray's ill again'. My Mum would say. And the music. My Dad's harmonica. *Danny Boy*. *Galway Bay*. Black 78s. And, of course, all the Priests.

From 'Across the Water' by Liz Niven, in *Irishness in Modern Scottish Writing* (Argyll, 2000).

My father was born in Glasgow in 1908. His father, Ned O'Malley, came over from Castlebar in County Mayo at the turn of the century. Ned, faced with the 'Oh' of anti-Irish sentiment from prospective employers – 'Oh, Malley, no work for you' – decided to drop it and his kids became plain 'Maley'. James – henceforth 'Daddy' – was brought up in Stevenson Street in the Calton, where he attended St Alphonsus. Daddy's daddy died in 1929, aged fifty-three. We don't even have a picture. All I know is that he had a fifty-inch chest and worked outside in all weathers all his days.

From 'Across the Water' by Willy Maley in *Irishness in Modern Scottish Writing* (Argyll, 2000).

The following two extracts are from young British women who are from Asian backgrounds.

I don't know how to start to describe myself. I feel identity-less, but very unique ... Maybe a potted personal history would help to describe me.

My parents are east African, their parents are Indian; I was born in Wales. So I was brought up by brown parents, with brown values, in a white middle-class community. I went to a white middle-class girls' private school and I had brown skin, short Western hair, western clothes, eastern name, western friends. So I guess I'm in an identity wasteland.

I used to insist I was Welsh, rather than say that I was Indian or East African Asian or British or of Asian descent. It was easier to say Welsh, because there isn't a stereotype of a brown Welsh person. Now I will only agree to being me.

From 'Set Yourself Free' by Salima Dhalla in Telling It Like it Is: Young Asian Women Talk (The Women's Press, 1997).

I am a fifteen year old Gujarati speaking girl, practising the Hindu religion. My family is originally from India, but both my parents were born in Uganda, Africa.

From 'A Ugandan Indian in Britain' by Niksha Thakrar, in Telling It Like It Is: Young Asian Women Talk (The Women's Press, 1997).

Reflecting

With a partner, **look over** these four extracts again.

● Which one appeals to *you* most? Why?

● Which of the extracts do *you* think tells you most about the writer? Why do you think that is?

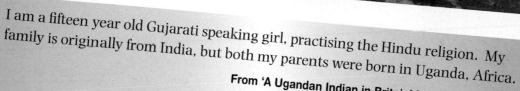

Writing it down

Try one or both of these exercises. Your teacher will tell you what you have to do.

- **Write** a paragraph about *your parents* and/or grandparents, saying who they were, where they came from, what jobs they did, where they lived.

- **Write** a paragraph about *yourself*, saying how you see yourself and how others see you. (Look again at Salima Dhalla's words for an example if you're not sure how to do this.)

Going even deeper

Writing about a talent or skill

I have been very musical almost since I was born. My mum says that when I was two, I was at nursery singing and holding a stone as if it was a microphone. From then Mum taught me Indian musical scales on a keyboard, and I would learn more things by watching my mum and dad. ... By the age of seven I was playing the tambourine at performances.

From 'Singing Star' by Annapurna Mishra in **Telling It Like It Is: Young Asian Women Talk** (The Women's Press, 1997).

Write about *a skill or talent* which is important to you and which you have developed over your life. It might be music, drama, sport, cooking or gymnastics, or anything else, big or little. Show what effect this still has on your life.

Going deeper still

Exploring your past through the senses

Here is an example of autobiographical writing where the author has used the sense of smell to describe a place she remembers.

I woke this morning with the smell of my auntie's house as sharp and real as if I was there, climbing the stair to their door. The smell started at the foot of the stair, getting stronger as you climbed, till you opened the door to the house, never locked, and shouted "It's me!" along the narrow lobby. It was a different smell from our house though equally familiar; stewed tea, an everlasting pot of soup, my uncle Pat's room with its furniture impregnated with smoke and the big press, stuffed full of mysterious junk.

Describe a place *you* remember in one or two paragraphs using a sense other than sight. In other words, use smell, touch, sound or taste, or a mixture of them. But *no* pictures.

Writing it down

In this section on autobiographical writing you have already written some short pieces about aspects of yourself. Now try to **write** a longer piece (this is called **extended writing**) by lengthening one or more of these pieces in a particular way, adding more ideas or exploring your ideas in more depth. Remember to put in **thoughts** and **feelings** as well as facts.

To help you, here are some suggestions:

- **A vivid childhood memory** – *you could use your work on senses to make this more vivid*

- **My talent or skill** – *you could use your work on senses and the family to make this more interesting*

- **Me and my family** – *you could include some of your work on names as well as family*

page 18

- **Who do I think I am?** *You could use some of your work on names, family and/or talents.*

These are just a few of the hundreds of particular ways you might write about yourself. Why not invent your own?

And finally...

See Visual Workpoints V3, V16, V18 and V19 for examples of *bibliography*.

Do you think these pieces of writing have helped you to understand who you are better than before? What else would be needed? Talk it over with a partner.

5 Pittin it in Scots

Take things easy!

'Take things easy!' is 'Soss!' in Scots.

Lairnin tae write in a new leid (*language*) can be gey (*very*) difficult. Even if ye're a really guid speaker o Scots, ye mibbe havenae *written* it down before.

There's different ways tae spell Scots an some folk use mair Scots words than other folk. Fir example, we could hae used 'afore' insteid o 'before', or 'doon' insteid o 'down' in the last but one **sentence**.

So dinnae worry. Yaise (*use*) as much or as little Scots as ye like in the wark that follaes. Spell it as ye fancy an as the words soon (*sound*) on yer lips. An aye (*always*) hae some fun (*daffery*). Richt?

Startin tae scrieve (*write*) in Scots

See Scots for Bairns

Monie year ago, afore the eighteenth century when **English** dictionaries started tae appear, English words could be spelt in different ways juist like Scots nooadays. Guid news for aw (*all*) the bairns at scuils lairnin Southron (*English*) in thon times!

There are noo guid Scots dictionaries, maistlie frae the twentieth century. At the moment, they gie us several choices o Scots spellin, for Scots hasnae settled. It's a leid (*language*) wi monie **dialect**s fand frae Shetland tae the Borders, an across the sea in Northern Ireland where Scots moved tae bide (*live*) in times gone by.

Glossary

Dialect: (also called a variety)
A language obviously different from related languages in its accent, words and their use, e.g. Geordie, Doric, standard English, Bajan etc. .
Accent:
A distinctive way of pronouncing words often associated with a region, a country, or part of a country e.g. American accent, Aberdonian accent etc.

Hae ye scrieved in Scots afore? If so, **discuss** in class hoo *difficult* or *easy* ye fand it.

Translatin intae Scots can be a good starter exercise tae get yersel comfortable an confident aboot usin written Scots. This kinna writin, insteid o makin up a whole short story, for example, means that ye're no worryin aboot creatin a new story at the same time as strugglin tae scrieve in whit micht be a new way. An, of course, while ye're translatin ye're lairnin the leid.

Mibbe yer teacher wad enjoy tryin this oot tae! Wark first of all wioot a Scots dictionary. It wad be helpfu mibbe but is no really necessar for this wark.

Some sentences for pittin intae Scots

1 There isn't anything to do.

2 I haven't got any sheep.

3 I have to go shopping.

4 He was frightened of the bull.

5 I cannot eat potatoes and turnips.

6 You shouldn't go down that street.

7 The little girl knew there was a burn next

8 It's very good to see friends from our past.

9 My father stayed in a farm on his own.

10 I would eat nothing at all rather than get fat.

I HAVENAE GOT ONIE YOWES

Mind (*remember*): as we said at the start, these sentences could be translated in monie ways. Ye could scrieve some o the **word**s in Scots an leave some o them in English as ye'll see we oorsels dae. An why no? Scots and English have common, ancient roots – for starters baith are Germanic languages – an they can, an dae, share monie spellins thegither (*together*) as does Scots wi, for example, Norwegian, German and Icelandic. As ye ken, there's mair aboot this on the CD-ROM.

Whan ye've feenished see the end o this section for possible translations intae Scots.

Aboot choices

As mentioned above, there are different ways you will have chosen to spell words. You might also have left some words in English.

The possible translations shown at the end have sometimes used the very strong Scots used in the past when, apart from **Gaelic** speakers, just about everybody in Scotland spoke and wrote in Scots. For example, for sentence number 9 you might have said *on his ain*. Our use of *aw his lane* is slightly more unusual. In sentence number 7 you probably kept *next* instead of *neist*.

None of these mixtures of Scots and English is 'wrong'. Many of the older, stronger Scots spellings you might find in stories and poems. Some of these writings would be from the past but modern Scottish writers still enjoy using them.

Glossary

Gaelic
A Celtic language found mainly in Scotland and Ireland.

Movin up – translatin paragraphs

Thae **paragraphs** tell a wee story. Mind an **mak yer ain choices** aboot hoo much or hoo little Scots ye want to use. Mibbe wark wi a partner?

One day last week I was walking home from school and I met Duncan.

He said, 'Where are you going?'

And I shouted, 'I'm going to my Gran's. Do you want to come with me?'

Duncan said, 'Yes. I like your Gran.'

Tomorrow morning I'm going to stay with my Grandmother. She lives in Kirkcudbright with Grandfather. It's always good fun at Grandmother's house because she's got two cats, four dogs and some very big cows. I just hope the weather isn't too wet.

'Come in,' said Granny. 'It's good to see you.'

'Hello, Granny,' I said 'Do you remember meeting Duncan last week?'

'Yes, son. Of course I remember. Do you think I'm getting old?' asked Granny.

'No chance, Granny,' I laughed. 'You'll be around long after me, no doubt.'

'Well, don't bother me with those sad thoughts. Away through to the cupboard and you'll find some sweeties, boys.'

We could hear Granny singing a little song to herself as we sat down with a big bag of sweeties.

'Always remember, boys, you always get what you deserve if it's right for you.'

Duncan and I are always really confused with those sayings of Granny. She's got a few of them for every occasion!

STOP! Ye'll find translations into Scots efter the next bittie.

Possible translations for the sentence wark

1   There isnae ocht tae dae.

2   A havnae got onie yowes.

3   A hae tae gan fir the messages.

4   He wis feart o the bull.

5   A cannae eat tatties an neaps.

6   Ye shouldnae gan doon that street.

7   The wee lassie kent there wes a burn neist.

8   It's awfy guid tae see freens fae wir past.

9   Ma faither steyed in a ferm aw his lane.

10 A wid eat naethin ava raither nor get fat.

Are these like your translations? Or are they different? **Compare** yours wi neibours or mibbe wi the hail (*whole*) class.

Possible translations for the paragraph wark

Yin day last week A wis walkin hame fae the scuil an A met Duncan.

He said, 'Whaur are ye gan?'

An A shoutit, 'A'm gan tae ma Grannie's. Dae ye want tae come wi me?'

Duncan said, 'Ay, A like yer Gran.'

The morn's morn A'm gan tae stey wi ma Grannie. She bides in Kirkcudbright wi ma Grampa. It's ayeweys guid fun at ma Grannie's hoose fir she's got twa cats, fower dugs an a wheen o gey muckle coos. A jist hope the weather isnae ower wet.

'Come awa ben,' said Grannie. 'It's guid tae see yes.'

'Hello, Granny,' A said. 'Dae ye mind meeting Duncan last week?'

'Ay son. Of course A mind. Dae ye think A'm gan doon the brae?' speirit Grannie.

> 'Nae chance, Grannie,' A laucht. 'You'll be aroon lang efter me nae doot.'
>
> 'Weel dinna fash me wi thon dowie thochts. Awa ben tae the press an ye'll fin some sweeties, boys.'
>
> We could hear Grannie croonin a wee sang tae hersel as we sat doon wi a big sweetie-poke.
>
> 'Ayeweys mind, boys, whit's fir ye'll no gan by ye.'
>
> Duncan an me are aye jist fair bamboozled wi thae sayins o Grannie. She's got a wheen o them fir every occasion.

Are these like your translations? Or are they different? **Compare** yours wi neibours or mibbe wi the hail class.

Things tae mind

Although there are some choices of spellings, there are some rules about scrievin in Scots.

Apostrophes are not used to show a 'missing' letter because no letters are missing *in Scots*. For example, 'and' becomes 'an' (not *an'*) an 'getting' becomes 'gettin' (not *gettin'*).

Capitals are always used for 'I' as in *A* or *Ah*. Sometimes, writers still use I, as in English.

Sometimes, you don't translate a single word into another single word, instead a whole **phrase** needs altering. Look at *the morn's morn*, for example. What did this come from?

gan doon the brae – can you work out the English phrase?

Audio Workpoints A1, A3, A4 and A5 have texts in Scots, and the website page has a Scottish section

Scrievin it doon

Noo try writing a wee **short story** o yer ain. Yaise as little or as much Scots as ye like. Mind what we said aboot fowk mibbe spekkin in Scots an the rest o the story being in English. An ay hae daffery. Richt?

But if you dinnae feel ready for this, you could write a short paragraph in English and then translate it into Scots. Dinnae hae a rid face (*be ashamed*) daein this. Ye're startin tae lairn a new leid. Sae soss!

6 Writing a diary

Personal history

There are many famous diaries such as *The Diary of Anne Frank*, set in the wartime Netherlands, or *The Diary of Adrian Mole*, about the fictional, once teenage boy who keeps growing up, or *The Diary of a Country Lady* about bygone times and most beautifully illustrated. How many other diaries do you know? Diaries are human records. Reading them lets us get close to a life – perhaps our own ....

Glossary

Subject
The person, or topic, at the centre of a text or some form of enquiry; or the word in a sentence with which the verb agrees.

Informal
Relaxed, casual, not following rules (see formal).

Lay out
How texts, or parts of texts, are set out on a page or screen.

About diaries

Personal diaries – not the kind where you jot down times and days of appointments or meetings – are a kind of history, or a personal newspaper. Personal diaries are often private, kept in secret, hidden because they deal with relationships that the writer would not want the world – or even a close friend – to know about.

Because events are recorded by only one person, only one mind, producing this kind of diary certainly involves a special kind of writing. The words being used are different from other forms of writing especially in terms of **voice** – the person who's telling the story – and **subject** – is there a subject? Are diaries always written **informally**? The **target audience** is also unusual – diaries often have only one reader who is also the writer. And what about **lay-out**?

Writing your own diary

Do you keep a personal diary? What sort of things do you write in it? Just facts like 'I met John'? Or do you also confide your feelings to your diary, telling it things you would not want other people to find out? 'I met John who gave me a hard-luck story. I felt sorry for him because he'd lost all his money although I do think he's a miserable stupido.' Would John *really* want to know your private view of him?

Now **think** of a recent day in *your own life* and **write** about the events and the people in it. It will be easier to do this if you choose a very unusual day – a day that is a bit different from the normal sort.

It might have been a very good day when things happened that made you **very** happy. You might have been asked to play the lead role in the school play – *or* you might have got out of doing it altogether! It might have been an awful day – right from the moment you opened your eyes things began to go badly. You had a fight with your mum, missed the school bus, left your homework behind, lost some money, argued with your best friend. A real shocker of a day!

Make sure you include the things that happened to you, whatever they were, which made the day memorable *and* include your **feelings** about these events.

Swap your entry with a neighbour and check each other's diary. Are there any gaps in the information? Do you get a clear picture of *things that have happened* as well as how your neighbour **feels** about the day's events?

 If you think you're not getting a clear picture, ask a few questions. For example, if they've mentioned arriving at school but not how they felt (*bored/fed up/glad/terrified*) then ask them to add this in.

Someone else's diary

Mary's Diary

Here is an extract from Mary's diary.

Monday 3rd May

Ye'll never guess whit happent the day? Bruce spoke tae me! Aye, he did. Telt ye ye wouldnae believe it didn't A? We were walkin doon the corridor tae Maths, me an Marie, an he jist kinna appeared at ma elbow and he says, 'Theresa isn't it?' An A says 'Aye', wi ma heart thumpin like it wis gan tae burst aw ower the corridor flair. 'How dae you ken?' and he says, 'A've been watchin ye fir days an then A askt somebody'. Aw listen, it wis brilliant. That wis it. That wis aw he said. A cannae wait till the morra – A cannae get tae sleep fir thinkin aboot him wi his big blue eyes.

> **Tuesday 4th May**
>
> Boys! A cannae unnerstaun them. There wis me aw delightit yesterday. Then A sees him the day and whit does he dae? Walkt past me! Honestly, A couldnae believe it. Marie says, A've either tae forget him or ask him oot. Whit am A gan tae dae?

The above extract is taken from Mary's diary. You'll have noticed that she tells about things that happened, who she spoke to, what they said, but **also** what her *thoughts and feelings* are.

Read the extract carefully. Then **write** down in your jotter any actions or events that Mary was involved with, people she met or spoke to, and any thoughts she had about the things that happened to her on Monday and Tuesday.

You might write it like this, making the table big enough to fit your words.

Actions/Events (*things that happened to Mary*)	**Thoughts** (*how Mary feels about the day's events*)

Glossary

Standard English
A dialect of English written and spoken in one common (i.e. 'standard') form across the British Isles – and elsewhere – but spoken with many accents.
Voice
Sounds produced by the vocal organs and how words are uttered in a text or life.

Mary's diary is written in Scots. Sometimes, it's easier to tell your real feelings if you use the voice you speak with naturally – probably the best voice in which to write a diary. It might be Scots or Yorkshire or perhaps **standard English** with Indian or Chinese words added in. You know the sound of your own **voice**, don't you?

More from Mary's diary

Wednesday 5th May

It's the next day. The next instalment. **Discuss** in class, or in groups, or with a partner, the sort of things that *could* happen now that you know a bit about her life.

Mary's voice

Mary says 'Ye'll never guess whit happent the day' – who is she talking to when she uses 'Ye'll'? When we fill in our diary we often speak to it as if it's to a real person.

STOP!

Now **write** her diary for Wednesday. Write it in a *personal voice*. Use Scots, English, or whatever you fancy. What might happen to her on that day? Does she speak to Bruce again? Will they become friends? We can't wait to read it ...

Another person's diary

Gideon's diary

This extract is written in Shetlandic Scots and tells the thoughts of a young fisherman called Gideon. It is his first time on the *haaf nets*, a type of net fishing. In Shetlandic 'th' is replaced by 'd' – 'dis' not 'this.' If you are in difficulties read it aloud. It's much easier than it looks.

> **Beltane – 1st May**
>
> Dis diary was a present fae Aald Mam an Aald Daa becis dis wid be me first time at da haaf. I'm lookin forwirt tae it. It'll mak a change fae cetchin bait aa trowe da simmer!
>
> I'm gaein tae wirk on a sixern wi Uncle Rasmie, an me cousin Jim. Da rest o da boys ir Magnus Isnister, Gibby Hendry, an Alec Watt. Daa wis gaein ta come wi is, bit he wis feelin por, so Gibby is taen his place. He's fair scunnered it he's no been able ta win dis year. It's his ain faat fir no lookin whaar he wis gaein.
>
> I tink I'll feenish here fir da day. I hae ta rise aafil early da morn's mornin, dan awa tae da haaf.
>
> From 'Da Diary o Gideon Hunter' by Peter Ratter from **The Kist/A'Chiste** (Scottish CCC/Nelson Blackie, 1996).

> A *sixern* is a boat rowed by six men.

Discuss with a partner
the *similarities* between this diary entry and Mary's? Look at the events Gideon is looking forward to, his thoughts and the voice he uses.

One more diary

Here is an extract from a story by Julie Bertagna

> You need to know that Skip and Kerrie have both run away from home and are living on the roof of a sky-scraper building in Glasgow. Restless is a cat.

> In one hand he held the sparkly disc. In the other his tatty notepad..
>
> The boy stood in her doorway.
>
> 'Sorry, didn't hear you knock.' Kerrie was crisp and polite. He hadn't.
>
> Ignores me all this time, she fumed, then comes barging in at midnight. He had some cheek.
>
> Skip was looking at her with the same flicker in his face she'd seen this morning.

'I brought over my sparkly.'

His voice was gruff as if he didn't use it much. The sound of it seemed to startle him even more than it did her. Kerrie wondered what on earth she was supposed to say. She'd better say something quick; he looked like he could just turn and go.

'Right. Well, come in then.'

Hardly encouraging, but what did he expect when he'd taken her totally by surprise? Then, she had done the same to him, hadn't she, barging up on to his roof without warning.

Skip shuffled in and stooped down beside the bedside candle. He placed the sparkly under its light. Then he spun it. Kerrie caught her breath as the dimness of the room scattered. Brilliant fireflies darted from the sparkly, stars exploded, rainbow lightning forked and spiked. Restless tried to pounce on the coloured lights and Kerrie held him back.

'It's – it's utterly crazy. You could watch it for hours.'

'I do,' said Skip.

'So you do.'

Kerrie picked up the disc when it was finally still. It was slightly larger than her hand and felt metallic. Underneath, she felt the tiny point in its centre that the sparkly spun on. Every fraction that she tilted it, the candlelight changed its colours and patterns. Blazing red and gold crashed greens and blue, then tinted to icy shades of purple and silver. She handed it back at last to save it from Restless.

'And I brought a poem,' said Skip.

'Oh. Ta.'

Once again, Kerrie was at a loss. She took the tatty notepad that he held out to her and saw an explosion of words scattered all over the page. then she saw that there was a kind of pattern to the scatter. It reminded her of something. Skip was looking at her edgily. She floundered for a response. It was unlike any poem she'd ever seen.

From **The Spark Gap** by Julie Bertagna (Mammoth, 1996).

Putting it in writing

The two people in this extract are Kerrie and Skip. You're going to **write** *either* Skip's *or* Kerrie's diary for that day. Decide whose diary you'd like to write.

Read the extract again imagining *you* are Kerrie *or* Skip. Try to see the events through their eyes. **Discuss** in class or in groups, the sort of emotions felt by Skip and Kerrie. You need to get inside their heads and imagine how they felt.

For example, if you are Kerrie, her diary might begin with *'I was mad this morning. Skip just walked into my doorway without knocking...'* or Skip might write, *'Guess what happened today. Another strange meeting with that girl Kerrie...'*

By the end of the diary entry, decide whether they are still friends. (Did Kerrie tell Skip his poetry writing wasn't daft at all? Or did they fall out?)

Now try to write Kerrie or Skip's diary page for this day. After you've finished, read out your version to the class or your group. You might want to read this very fine book to see what does happen next!

7 Creating atmosphere

Revealing character

> *How* a novelist, or film-maker, or radio scriptwriter – or anybody telling a story for that matter – brings you into the narrative is a very important part of what makes you interested in that narrative. It is all part of making the atmosphere of the narrative. Helping to create the atmosphere are the characters who live in the story's world. How are they made?

Glossary

Novel
A long piece of fiction about the lives and experiences of a number of characters (see short story). A novelist is a person who has written a novel, or novels.

Narrative
A text which tells a story e.g. a novel, an opera, a TV soap opera.

Atmosphere
A feeling or mood.

Characters
Persons or beings in a fictional text and/or, especially as a singular noun, their qualities.

A young boy visits a graveyard. Here is an extract, one tiny part of an exciting, interesting novel.

My footprints track across the faint dew still lying on the grass. My boots crunch heavily on the hard gravel path, and I'm talking to myself as I walk, school bag bumping on my back. But the residents lodged on either side of these avenues won't complain about the noise.

They're dead.

Every one of them.

Their headstones march beside me. I stop to look at one of my favourites. A weaver. There is a carving of a leopard with a shuttle in its mouth. The animal's head is black with age, its stone roar a silent echo in a grey Scottish kirkyard. The leopard used to be on the crest of the Guild of Weavers. My dad told me.

Early morning mist comes creeping between the gravestones. I shiver. It's because I'm cold though, not scared.

Not yet.

I touch the old tinker's grave. A ram's horns and crossed spoons. That's how I know a tinker is buried there. The carvings and designs on the stones tell you. They all mean something. My dad told me to listen and I would hear the crackle of the gypsies' campfire, the black pot swinging just above the flames.

I wish words on paper were as easy to read and understand.

From 'Whispers In The Graveyard' by Theresa Breslin (Heinemann, 1986).

We learn a lot about the graveyard and about the boy's character – what he's like. How does Theresa Breslin do this? Here are some of the ways she does it and you're going to learn from her how to do this for yourself. This isn't copying. It's called learning from others – *the best way to learn*.

Step one – use detail to build up a picture

The author picks out two graves to describe:

- a weaver's grave
- a tinker's grave.

With a partner, **make a note** of *all* the information Theresa Breslin gives you about each of these graves. Set each fact that you've discovered on a separate line on your paper.

Step two – use your senses

Three senses that you could use:

- seeing
- hearing
- touching

Look at the notes you made for each of the graves. Beside each one **write** down which of the senses *you* think is being used. (**Hint**: Remember you can *see* and *touch* carvings.)

Step three – choose your words carefully

Glossary

Verb
The word in a sentence that shows movement, action or conditions.

The author has chosen her words with great care to describe the scene. Her choice of **verb**s is particularly effective. She often uses words which help us to hear the sound being made: *'My boots* **crunch** *heavily on the hard gravel path.'*

When you say *crunch* out loud you can hear the noise made by the boy's feet. Say it out loud. Can you think of other words that have the same sounds as the sounds they describe? **Make a list** of five or so, quickly, with a partner.

Find the **paragraph** which starts, *'I touch the old tinker's grave.'* Can you find a word in this paragraph which suggests the sound of the object?

pages 51-60

This piece of **figurative language** where the sound suggests the meaning of the word, is called **onomatopoeia**. Say the word three or four times to a partner, making sure you get the pronunciation right.

Glossary

Onomatopoeia
Where the sound of a word suggests its meaning e.g. hush, roar, rummle.
Figurative language
When a writer or talker creates a picture by using words in special ways, e.g. metaphors and similes.
Metaphor
When one thing is said to be another to help the reader better imagine what is being described e.g. The Moon, a white skull, rose above the horizon (see figurative language).
Simile
Figurative language in which one thing is said to be *like* or *as* another e.g. he's like a zombie watchin yon telly.

Step four – use figurative language

Use of onomatopoeia is one way of using **figurative language**. But there are many ways. Comparing one thing to an other thing is one of the main ways. Let's look at Theresa Breslin's use of figurative language.

> The animal's head is black with age, its stone roar a silent echo in a grey Scottish kirkyard.

Here Theresa Breslin compares the *stone roar* of the lion to a *silent echo*. As you know, this piece of figurative language is called a metaphor. What perhaps you don't know is that the picture the metaphor makes inside our heads is called an **image**.

Think about it. Even though they come from outside and are made from words, we still feel that these pictures, these images, are happening inside our heads. We have the same feeling about the pictures we see on TV, films and in photographs, for example. For this reason these **mass media** are also said to be made out of **images**.

Back to our example of figurative language…

> The animal's head is black with age, its stone roar a silent echo in a grey Scottish kirkyard.

This image is very complicated, so let's look at it again, this time in detail. Take *stone roar* first.

A roar is a sound. How can a *roar* be made of stone? And what about *silent echo*? An echo is also a sound. What does the author mean when she says it is *silent*? Can you solve this puzzle by talking it over either with a partner or in the whole class?

On the next page are some **nouns** and **adjectives**. Can you put one noun and an adjective together to make an interesting **metaphor**, an interesting **image**? Be prepared to explain what you mean so put your image into a **sentence** to make things clear.

Glossary

Noun
The word used to describe a person, a place, an object, a feeling or quality or a collection of things.
Adjective
A word that describes a noun or pronoun.

Nouns	Adjectives
ice	green
rain	fiery
bread	jewelled
girl *or* boy	ghostly
dream	still
bus	tangled

Compare your images with a partner. Then choose *one*, the best one, to present to the class. Be prepared to say why you think it is a good image and read out the sentence where it appears. The whole class will then choose the one it thinks is best. Good luck!

Step five – reveal character

'Whispers in the Graveyard' is told in the **first person**. That means that the author has written it as if the boy is telling us the story.

The author has told us a lot about the character of the boy, though she does not actually *say* these things directly. Instead, she shows us by the things *he says and does*.

Look at the following statements about the boy. With a partner **decide** whether *you* think they are **true** or **false**.

1 The boy likes the graves.

2 The boy is scared being in the graveyard.

3 The boy hardly ever goes there.

4 The boy is imaginative.

5 The boy listens to his Dad.

6 The boy finds reading books easy.

7 The boy likes the sounds of words.

Put the heading **true** in your jotter and **write** down the *true statements*, leaving a space between them. Forget the other statements for the moment. Beside each truth **write** down the evidence: write down what the author told us in the passage which makes *you* think it is true.

Put the heading **false** in your jotter and **write** down the *false statements*, leaving a space between them. Beside each one **write** down the reasons *you* think it is false.

> **Glossary**
>
> **First person**
> Used where the speaker or writer is referring to her or himself, using words like I, me, mine etc. (see third person).

Now put it in writing

Here are a number of activities based on the work you've just done. Your teacher may suggest which of these you should do, or give you a choice. Your teacher may want you to do them all!

Creating atmosphere

Think of a place you know well. It could be a place outside, such as a garden, beach, field, or somewhere inside, like your room at home or this classroom.

Choose *one* feature or object in the place – for example, a tree or plant, your desk, your bed.

Step one – use detail

Write a paragraph describing the object by using *descriptive detail*. No images, please, just straightforward description.

Step two – use your senses

Use *one* of the five sense of **hearing, smell, touch, taste** and **sight** to describe the object.

Step three – choose your words

Take time to choose good words for your descriptions.

Step four – use figurative language

Use an image to describe the object.

Now look at the paragraph you have written. Which description did you like best? Why?

Step five – revealing character

Think of a place you know well. It could be a place outside, such as a garden, beach, field, or somewhere inside, like your room at home or the classroom. It could, in other words, be the same place you used earlier.

Make a list of the *main features* of the place. For example, if you were describing a classroom, you would list the size and shape of the room, how it is decorated, the number and size of windows, furniture, etc.

Now pick *one* of the characters from the panel below. **Write** using a first person narrative *two paragraphs*. As this character you have come into the place, and are sitting or standing looking around you.

(Remember: *Don't write down, or in any way make it obvious, which character you have picked.*)

You have to show what the character is like by describing:

- how s/he moves
- how s/he speaks
- the things s/he notices in the place
- what s/he feels about the place.

Use one of these characters

- I'm a very shy person. I hate to stand out in a crowd or draw attention to myself. I like quiet places. I notice a lot.

- Me? I'm confident and friendly, but not loud. I'm a cheerful person who likes to talk to other people. I don't like being on my own. I'm active and like to move about.

- I'm clumsy, always bashing into things and having accidents. I suppose I'm a bit of a daydreamer and don't really pay much attention to what's going on round about me. I'm more interested in what's going on inside my own head.

- I like to be the boss. I hate being told what to do. If anyone gives me hassle I just give it back to them. I have very definite likes and dislikes. I get bored easily.

- I'm laid-back. Easy-going. Love music. Prefer being out of doors.

After you've written your paragraphs swop them with another pupil. Each of you should try to work out which character the other has written about.

If your partner was right, ask them what it was about your paragraphs that showed them the character.

If your partner thought it was a different character, ask them what they thought would have made it clearer.

Now you can:

- *either* rewrite your original, trying to improve it
- *or* try the exercise again, using a different character
- *or* you may wish to continue with the piece of writing, adding more paragraphs. If you do, try to include at least one other character.

8 Openings

Starting a short story or novel

pages 7-14

The **opening** of a short story or novel must get the reader's attention. Usually, it gives some idea of **where** and **when** the story is set, **who** is telling the story, **who** the main characters are, and what kind of story it is going to be. There are many different ways of opening a story...remember the keys?

Glossary

Short story
A text, always fiction, of perhaps less than 1000 words, usually more.

Novel
A long piece of fiction about the lives and experiences of a number of characters.

Some examples of openings

Opening A

I don't think my mum's fit to be a parent, really I don't. Every morning it's the same, every single morning. I'm standing by the door with my coat on, ready to go. School starts at nine and it's already eight-forty or even later, and she's not ready. She's not even nearly ready. Sometimes she isn't even dressed.

From **Crummy Mummy and Me** by Anne Fine (Puffin, 1989).

Opening B

It was silent and dark and the children were afraid. They huddled together, their backs to an outcrop of rock. Far below them, in the bed of the gully, a little stream flowed inland – soon to peter out in the vastness of the Australian desert. Above them the walls of the gully climbed smoothly to a motionless sky.

From **Walkabout** by James Vance Marshall (Puffin, 1980).

Opening C

Great drops of rain burst in the shape of fried eggs and streamed messily down the tall windows that ran the length of the school gym hall.

Jerry sat on a pile of spongy gym mats, thinking what an unwatery sound it was as the rain crescendoed to full battering pitch.

From **The Spark Gap** by Julie Bertagna (Mammoth, 1986).

Opening D

'All right,' said Nicholas. 'You're fed up. So am I. But we're better off here than at home.'

'It wouldn't be as cold as this,' said David.

'That's what you say. Remember how it was last time we moved? Newspapers on the floor, and everyone sitting on packing cases. No thanks!'

From **Elidor** by Alan Garner (Lions, 1992).

pages 67-72

Work with a partner or in a small group.   **Answer** the following *questions* about the four openings.

1 Three of the openings are **third person narratives** and one is told in the **first person**. Find them.

> **Glossary**
>
> **Third person**
> Where the speaker or writer is referring to others using words like she, her, he, him, it, they, them etc. (see first person).
> **First person**
> Where the speaker or writer is referring to her or himself, using words like I, me, mine etc. (see third person).

> **Glossary**
>
> **Monologue**
> One person speaking, usually to an audience, in a narrative of some kind.
> **Audience**
> The person or persons reading, watching or listening to something (see target audience).

2 What do you learn in each opening about:

- the place?
- the time of day?
- the weather?
- the feelings of the character(s)?
- anything else you think might be important?

3 Which of the openings used:

- dialogue?
- **monologue**?
- description?

As you can see, each writer starts their story in a different way.

When you are writing your own stories, it is a good idea to think carefully about, and perhaps try out, different ways of starting the story. Experiment to see which one is best.

 STOP!

Putting it in writing

Try one, or both, of these writing tasks.

1 **Rewrite** Opening A in the *third person*. (The main character's name is Minna.)

2 **Rewrite** Opening D *without* using dialogue.

Which of these versions do you prefer ? Why?

Suggesting not telling

Each opening is a very short paragraph, yet the writers have suggested a lot of information. Writers often **suggest** things rather than *telling us directly*. Suggesting can be a more interesting way of telling a story than telling it outright. For example, let's look again at Opening D to see what it suggests.

We can work out that the two boys are probably outside as it is cold, and they've gone out because they are moving house. We also know it is not the first time they have moved. We can work out that they're probably brothers. Yet the author hasn't actually told us any of these things *directly*, merely suggested them through the dialogue.

> **Glossary**
>
> **Plot**
> What happens in a story.
> **Dialogue**
> The words used by characters, usually in scripts and fiction, *and* a conversation between people.

Writing it down

Now try an exercise in suggesting. Choose either (or both) of the following **plots** and **write** a few paragraphs using **dialogue**, trying to *suggest* the information rather than saying it directly.

Plot one

Two sisters, Nadia and Aliya, are on their way to visit their grandmother, who lives a short distance away from them. Nadia is older than Aliya. **Write** their *dialogue*, trying to show that they are *not* looking forward to going to see their grandmother.

Plot two

Justin and Derek are waiting outside the Head Teacher's office. Derek has been sent there to be punished for bad behaviour and Justin has been sent to get a certificate for good work in his reading project. **Write** the *dialogue* between them, showing they are friends.

Compare your work with a partner, and discuss its merits and problems.

Write your own opening

Audio Workpoint A1 has the opening to a short story in Scots

Write the opening – and maybe the whole – of a **short story**. In either case, pay particular attention to the opening.

Again, compare your work with a partner, and discuss its merits and problems.

9 Choosing the right word

Making a word picture

pages 36-42

Writers have ways of describing a scene so carefully we can really see it. How do they do this? As well as creating atmosphere and characters, they also choose **good words**.

Read over this extract with a partner. As you do so *try to picture* the scene very clearly in your mind's eye. Then read it *again*.

You need to know that Maura is 11 years old. She lives in Belfast in the recent past. Between her family and 'The Troubles' life for her is not easy. Sometimes she wishes that someone, her guardian angel, for example, would give a helping hand...

This extract is available for DARTs techniques.

Suddenly they heard it, and the hearts seemed to stop in all of them. A noise like the bark of a dog outside. But it wasn't a dog. It was a human voice barking out an order. And before they could do anything at all, there was a crashing, splintering noise from the hall. In the next split second came heavy, running steps out at the back, the thud of boots as men dropped from the high alley wall. A rifle butt crashed through the glass panel in the kitchen door, and, before the glass had settled on the floor, the door was flung open.

More uniformed men, burst in. The first one thrust Ma aside as they ran through the kitchen. Another bark, louder and closer this time, from the hall. Ma had leapt to her feet, and so had Angela, the dustpan adding its clatter to the racket of hard boot-steps and shouts and the tinkle of more glass. Maura, half stunned as she was, thought, 'There goes the front room window – the one overlooking the street.' The next thing, she and Angela were bumping into each other as they tried to rush through the kitchen door at the same moment behind the khaki backs. Angela got through first.

The little hall was crammed with soldiers. The front door and the door to the living room had been burst open – the front door was hanging by one hinge. Soldiers were pouring in. Above their heads, Maura could see another, clambering in through the smashed window over the back of the sofa, his rifle barrel catching on the net curtains and dragging them down. Her Da, Kieran and the other three men were somewhere in there. Trapped. And she couldn't get to them.

She fought, pushing and struggling, but the backs were too many, too tightly wedged, too strong. She heard her own voice screaming, 'Da! Da! Don't hurt my daddy!' and her mother behind her screaming louder, 'Don't shoot! Don't anybody shoot!' And the barking voice, still barking, loud unmeaning sounds which only a soldier can understand.

Then the shots rang out – two, almost at the same moment. They exploded in the little house as shatteringly as the bomb had exploded in the street.

From **Maura's Angel** by Lynne Reid Banks (Heinemann, 1986).

Putting it in writing

Working with your partner, show by **underlining** or by using a highlighter pen *on your photocopy* those words or phrases *you both think* give a really clear idea of what is happening. These will be the words which help you to imagine the scene.

Then, using a different kind of line, or colour of highlighting, mark any words which are used for *sounds*.

Compare notes with another pair and be prepared to say *why* you've decided to mark certain words.

Glossary

Adverb
A word that tells us more about a verb or adjective.

Technical terms

It's useful to know the names for the words and phrases which help to make a piece of language – written or spoken – work. We're going to look at four of these terms. One is explained. If you don't know the others check in the Glossary and/or talk to your teacher.

Again with your partner (or in a larger group of four) decide which words in the extract are:

- adjectives
- adverbs
- verbs
- onomatopoeia.

pages 51-59

Draw four columns in your jotter like this. Look at the passage from *Maura's Angel* and add to the examples here.

Adjectives	Verbs	Adverbs	Onomatopoeia
e.g. splintering	e.g. exploded	e.g. shatteringly	e.g. tinkle

When you've finished **discuss** with your teacher and/or the whole class why these words work well.

Telling a story to others

Imagine you're lying in bed late at night. You're going to use this setting for the beginning of a story. You find yourself wide awake in the middle of the night. You're going to try to help your **audience** imagine the scene very clearly, to share with them just how scared you feel.

Think about some exact words and use onomatopoeia to describe how you get out of bed, go into the kitchen, peer through the windows, and so on – that is, if you can bear to get out of bed at all! Jot some words down to help you remember the story but *don't write it – yet!*

Please *don't* have any horrible monsters waiting for you because that's just a **cliché**. But do give the **impression** that there is something else there – either inside or outside the house! Something you can't see or hear – but you *know* it's there. It will help if you think very clearly about a time when you have actually done this. Think how you might make your story *really* scary.

page 46

Try **suggestion**, rather than telling your story directly.

When you've thought the task through, tell your partner *your story* as scarily as possible – using only words. You each have *five minutes* to tell your stories in turn, so you don't have any time to waste. Now, after this practice run, cluster into fours and see who can tell the best story in the group. Decide why the best story was best.

Glossary

Cliché
Words or ideas that have become boring through overuse.

In class, **talk** about why some stories are better than others.

Can you work out some keys for making this kind of scary story really interesting? When you've made your keys (using the keys in Chapter 2 to guide you), **write** them into your jotter so that you can look at them again when you're next going to write this kind of story.

pages 11-14

Writing it down

Now **write** *your* story down remembering all the bits that seemed to work – that seemed to have had the scariest effect on your listeners. Use them in your writing, and perhaps add to them.

> **Glossary**
>
> **Information**
> Knowledge transmitted *and/or* received, usually about a particular matter.

Remember your **target audience**. You are writing for friends and you're trying to frighten them with your writing, so make your description very clear and easy for them to imagine. Give them lots of **information**. Use **figurative language**.

Things to remember when you're writing

- Describe what happened in *as much detail* as you can.

- Show effects on your **characters** by *including their feelings*.

- Use different lengths of **sentences** to *create suspense*. Shorter ones are sometimes good.

- Use **onomatopoeia**, **adjectives**, **adverbs** and *exact* **verb**s

If you have time...

When you've both finished, exchange your story with a partner then **talk** about the parts of your stories which seemed to work best, and those which didn't work at all. Try to work out *why* some worked, and others didn't.

10 Imagery part one

Novels and short stories

pages 39-40

When a writer creates pictures through words, she or he is making images. **Imagery** is found in novels and short stories, in newspapers, in magazines and advertisements. Images are everywhere. Written images are made by using figurative language.

See Visual Workpoint V17

Look at the following **paragraph**. It comes from the beginning of a chapter in **The House on the Hill**, a novel by Eileen Dunlop (Canongate, 1989).

What images or pictures can you see? **Write** down *your* ideas by yourself in a jotter. Your teacher will discuss your ideas with you when you have done this.

Now it was November. Fireworks had their season, wet yellow leaves lay like skin on the pavements of Knightshill, and glistening black trees were everywhere adrip. Each afternoon, fawnish fog slipped up the river, blanketing the low-lying parts of the city, and coiling lazily upwards into Wisteria Avenue. The old Gothic mansions took on the appearance of castles in a ghost story, with their pointed roofs and ornamental turrets wrapped in gauzy scarves of mist. In the garden of The Mount, every tree wept sadly, and Jane took to filling hot-water bottles for the children before she went off to bed.

How did you do? We think that images are everywhere in this part of the story.

The writer suggests that the leaves *lay like skin on the pavements*. She is creating a picture which suggests that the leaves are clinging so tightly to the pavement they make a skin like the one that covers a person's bones.

What about *blanketing*? What do we use blankets for? We use them to cover ourselves in bed. So a word like *blanketing* carries with it the idea that blankets keep us warm on winter nights and we wrap ourselves up in them. Notice that the time of the story is November.

 These are not the only examples of images in this extract. Believe it or not, there are *more*! Can you find them? Exchange your images with a partner.

Talking about images

Some images we noticed were: *castles in a ghost story*, *wrapped in gauzy scarves of mist*, and *every tree wept sadly*. How would you explain them, not one by one, but as a group? Work with a partner to **explain** these images. What effect is the author creating? How does she do it?

Eileeen Dunlop is suggesting that the fog is everywhere, completely covering parts of the city, making the buildings, streets and open spaces impossible to see. She is also making us feel the effect, isn't she?

What other image is used in the paragraph to suggest the idea of the fog surrounding something?

Using images

Images come in chains

Think about it. These kinds of images are always used when writers want to describe something in an interesting way. To do so they compare one thing to another – leaves to skin, fog to blankets, and so on. These are either **metaphors** or **similes**. Such comparisons make pictures – images – in our minds. You've also found out they sometimes come in groups, or chains of linked images. Why do you think this is? How are they linked? **Talk** about this in class.

Here is another extract to look at. What images or pictures do you see here? Work with a partner, **jot** down ideas in your jotters, and your teacher will discuss them with you after you have studied the extract.

This extract is taken from a novel by Marlene Fanta Shyer. The novel is called **Welcome Home Jellybean** (Collins Educational, 1984). A boy called Neil is on stage playing the piano at a school concert.

I began to play, concentrating with every spark plug in my head, letting my fingers remember each plink and plunk, getting the horsepower into my hands, and, like Dad had told me, going easy on the right pedal. I relaxed . . .it was working! My fingers took over and zipped along like they belonged to someone else, maybe **Tchaikovsky**. The keyboard felt like velvet and the tempo was perfect. The cramps disappeared; I was really proud of myself.

Glossary

Internet
Worldwide information highway made from inter-connected computer networks.
URL
(Uniform Resource Locator) An Internet address e.g. the URL for Turnstones is www.turnstones-online.co.uk

Resources

Tchaikovsky was a nineteenth century Russian composer of classical music. You can find out more about him on the Internet at this URL:
w3.rz-berlin.mpg.de/cmp/tchaikovsky.html

So where are the images here? How about the description of *every spark plug in my head*, the idea of *getting the horsepower into my hands*, and the picture of *going easy on the right pedal*?

If you look closely at these images, you can see one idea which repeats to form a chain.

Hint: what things found everywhere – in the Western world at least – do you associate with spark plugs, horsepower and pedals?

Okay. Too easy, that question, wasn't it? All of them are examples of language associated with cars. What do 'spark plugs' do? What is their job? What does 'horsepower' refer to? What is the author referring to when she makes mention of the 'pedals'? Could this be an accelerator pedal? And what has all this to do with playing a piano?

Discuss these ideas, and the idea of a chain of images, with your partner. Together you can make notes about the ideas contained in these images or pictures.

pages 36-42

There are many pieces of **figurative language** which make images. Some you may have met before. The most important of them are **metaphors** and **similes**. But you might also think of **personification** and **onomatopoeia**.

Personification, onomatopoeia, metaphors and similes are all examples of figurative language! They always add colour and feelings to a piece of writing. If necessary, talk about them with your teacher.

You should now, with your teacher, look back at the two extracts in this chapter and try to 'label' their images. This is a way of making sure you can remember the names of the figures of speech used by Eileen Dunlop and Marlene Fanta Shyer. Can you? Can you find any other examples, perhaps in this book or another?

> **Glossary**
>
> **Personification**
> Where an object or idea is spoken of as if it had human qualities, e.g. the wind moaned through the trees.

Putting it in writing

Write either a *short story*, or the *opening* paragraphs of that story, about one of the following events. You should use as many images as you think is necessary to make pictures in the reader's mind.

- Storm at sea
- The perfect meal
- Superman visits your school
- A new baby arrives in your family
- Your pet goes missing
- A helicopter crash
- A burning house

Read your stories in a group and decide which is best. Vote on it. The winners from each group should read their stories aloud to the whole class. Discuss which of these is best, voting on it. Remember you don't have to choose one single winner. Try to work out what makes the winning stories better than others.

11 Imagery part two

Pictures in poetry

For many people, word images and figurative language (and the pictures they make in our minds) are mostly associated with poetry. But imagery is used in *all* forms of writing, even in newspapers. If you turn the pages of your **Daily Record**, or **Sun**, or **Herald**, or **Press and Journal** you'll find plenty of examples of imagery in them. But it *is* true that you'll find regular examples of imagery in poems, and sometimes in songs.

pages 47-50

pages 10-12

When you read a poem in class, you'll find your teacher will want to ask you about **what** makes a poem *interesting, clever* or maybe just plain *brilliant*, and **how** the **what** works! Remember the keys?

You might have to think about:

- imagery
- word choice
- dialect
- rhythm and rhyme
- structure

These five things are a few of what are called the **techniques** (the ways of doing things – also called the **devices**) used by poets when they write.

At the moment, we're interested in the first one on the list: **imagery**. So, here are a few images from poems to discuss. You should work with a partner. As well as answering the questions on each of the poems, you should *always* ask yourselves if you think the images, the pictures, are *interesting*.

Glossary

Rhythm
Sound patterns made by emphasising words or syllables in a text.

Rhyme
Usually in poetry, when the last sound of a line (or, more rarely, a sound anywhere in the line) repeats one found earlier.

Syllable
One of the sounds that make a word, e.g. in Auchterarder, *auch, ter, ard* and *er* are all syllables.

Some poems

page 60

Work on the following four exercises with a partner, or in a group. Your teacher will decide on this, and whether you are to do all or some. You'll find a panel with some of *our* **interpretations** farther on.

Interpretation is the searching for meanings.

Exercise one

The first image is from a poem called **In the Snack Bar** by a Scottish poet, Edwin Morgan, describing a poor man who is both blind and deformed. At one point in the poem, Morgan says that the old man:

> . . . stands in his stained, beltless **gaberdine**
> like a monstrous animal caught in a tent. . .

Gaberdine is a loose, baggy overcoat made of this material, often worn by beggars.

- What is the poet suggesting by *like a monstrous animal?*

- What does he mean by the old man being *caught in a tent?*

- Can you name the figures of speech being used here?

From the same poem, the poet explains that for the old man:

> A few yards of floor are like a landscape. . .

- What does Morgan suggest about the size of the place by using the word landscape?

- Is this meant to be a real description?

- What does it tell us about the old man?

Exercise two

Vernon Scannell wrote a poem called **A Case of Murder**, in which he describes how a young boy of nine years old is scared by the family pet, a cat. He describes the cat as:

> ...a cat with round eyes mad as gold,
>
> Plump as a cushion with tucked in paws –
>
> ...
>
> A buzzing machine of soft black stuff. . .

Later in the poem, the small boy accidentally traps the cat in a door, just as it is trying to slip through. Scannell describes how...

> The cat, half-through, was cracked like a nut...

As with the previous example, try to explain what the images are that are being created.

- What comparisons are being made by the poet?

- What pictures are being made in your mind?

- What are the figure(s) of speech being used?

- Are they successfully used?

Exercise three

In his poem **My Parents Kept Me from Children who were Rough** (interesting title!) Stephen Spender writes that:

> My parents kept me from children who were rough
>
> And who threw words like stones. . .

Later in the poem he says that:

> I feared more than tigers their muscles like iron. . .

- What is the effect of the descriptions of words being thrown *like stones* and of *muscles like iron*?

- What does the word *tigers* tell you about the rough children, and about what the young Spender thought of them?

Exercise four

Another Scottish poet, Norman MacCaig, wrote a poem about a Brooklyn policeman called **Brooklyn Cop**. Brooklyn is a district in New York, in the USA. It's a place often thought of as violent and scary.

At one point in the poem, MacCaig describes the policeman as:

Built like a gorilla. . .

- What figure of speech is this?

- How do you know?

- What does the image tell you about the policeman?
  (Think of more than one answer.)

Looking back

With other pupils in the class *or* with the teacher, **discuss** your views, or the views of your group, on one or more than one of these texts. Explore disagreements. With an image, there are many possible **interpretations**. Why do you think this is?

Reading and writing poems

Here is a whole poem by Norman MacCaig. **Read** it aloud together in a group, two or three times, with different readers.

Then, still in the group, **find** the *metaphors*, *similes*, *onomatopoeia*, and *personifications* that give the poem some of its meanings. **Write** them down. Then try to work out **what** they mean. **Who** is observing the night? Finally, work out **what** the whole poem means. You should then be able to tell **how** readers of the poem are **supposed** to feel when they've read it. When you have reached some kind of agreement on the last two tasks **write** your findings down and **talk** about your discoveries in the class.

November night, Edinburgh

The night tinkles like ice in glasses.
Leaves are glued to the pavements with frost.
The brown air fumes at the shop windows,
Tries the door and sidles past.

I gulp down winter raw. The heady
Darkness swirls with tenements.
In a brown fuzz of cottonwool
Lamps fade up crags, die into pits.

Frost in my lungs is harsh as leaves
Scraped up on paths. I look up, there.
A high roof sails, at the mast-head
Fluttering a grey and ragged star.

The world's a bear shrugged in his den.
It's snug and close in the snoring night.
And outside like chrysanthemums
The fog unfolds its bitter scent.

Norman MacCaig

Glossary

Editing
The rearranging, and possibly rewriting, of parts of texts such as print, audio or visual materials to improve their content.

Finally, **write** a short poem containing at least *six* or *seven* images. You'll maybe have to do this several times, correcting, **editing** it, improving it. When you are happy with your poem sign it and pin it up in the classroom.

Remember: there is no such thing as a bad poem. All poems are like all people – including old men in snack bars, Brooklyn cops and rough children – all of them of equal value...

Some of our ideas about the images in the extracts

Example	Image of....	Figure of speech
Like a monstrous animal	Something horrible, ugly, hideous	simile
...caught in a tent	Coat is too big for him, hangs about him, is loose	metaphor
A few yards are like a landscape	Suggests that small distance is huge to him	simile
Built like a gorilla	Big, strong, dangerous, aggressive, an 'animal'	simile
Plump as a cushion	Fat, heavy, 'round'	simile
the cat...cracked like a nut	'broken', easily badly injured snapping noise like breaking bone(s)	simile onomatopoiea
buzzing machine	'Buzzing' is the purring sound being made by the cat, 'machine' makes it sound inhuman, cold, unfeeling, not a real living thing, therefore more scary	onomatopoiea again metaphor
threw words like stones	Said things which caused hurt, pain	simile
muscles like iron	Strong, tough, fit, 'hard', therefore dangerous	simile
tigers	Normally, suggests something fierce but Stephen Spender was more afraid of something else, wasn't he? What?	metaphor

12 Imaginative writing

Makin folk seem real

Ye've begun tae start stories, shape stories, create atmosphere in stories and write in Scots or English, or a mixture o baith. It's time tae add another exercise, tae pit them aw thegither an use everything ye've learned sae far tae mak folk mair 'real'. Words in this colour hae an owersettin (translation) at the end.

Read the followin extract frae a short story by Lavinia Derwent

'What are ye gaun to plant in't?' **speired** Mrs Erchie, wha wad raither hae been back in the tenement, hingin oot. 'Flooers?'

'Tatties', quo Erchie, wi the rotation o crops still whurlin aboot in his heid. 'An mebbe a **pickle** peas, an a handfu o **ingans** an twa-three collyflouers an a **wheen** neeps.'

'What aboot a palm-tree when ye're aboot it?' said Mrs Erchie, sarcastic-like.

Ah weel, **i the hinner-end**, it wes a kind o **mixty-maxty** that cam up, wi a guid **hantle** o weeds thrawn in; but Erchie wes as prood o his handiwark as if he had planted the Gairden o Eden single-handed. There wes only ae snag, apairt frae the weeds.

'**Speugs!**' quo Erchie, diggin up a divot an chuckin it at twae birds that had flewn in for their denners. 'I didna ken there were sae mony in the warld, an the **hale jing-bang** o them come **gallivantin** into *ma* gairden, peckin up ma peas, an makin a fair **slaister** o ma strawberries.' He had six strawberries, nae mair an nae less, but it wes aye something.

'I've a guid mind to get a haud o a gun.'

'Ye'd be better wi a **tattie-bogle**,' quo Mrs Erchie, **ruggin** up a dandylion.

'A tattie-bogle! Michty me! Whaur d'ye think I'd pit it? It wad need to be a gey sma ane, for I canna even get room for ma radishes,' said Erchie, **scartin his powe**, but ye could see he wes taen on wi the idea.

'Ye coud pit it on the path,' said Mrs Erchie (if ye coud ca it a path). 'I tell ye what, ye can have Mary-Ann. I'm feenished wi her.'

Erchie opened his een wide, an says he, '**Goveydick!** Whaever heard o a female tattie-bogle? Forby, Mary-Ann'll be far ower **perjinct** for **siccan** a job.'

'Oh weel, I've made the offer,' said Mrs Erchie, an **dichtit** her hands.

From **The Tattie-Bogle** by Lavinia Derwent
(Mak it New, The Mercat Press, 1995).

owersettin translation

speired asked

pickle few

ingans onions

wheen several

i the hinner-end in the end

mixty-maxty mixture

hantle large number

Speugs Sparrows

the hale jing-bang the whole lot

gallivantin going out (this is an English word!)

slaister a splashy mess

tattie-bogle scarecrow

ruggin tugging

scartin his powe scratching his head

Goveydick! Wow!

perjinct smart-looking

siccan such

dichtit rubbed clean

Addin actions

When ye're speakin tae somebodie, ye probably don't staun or sit wi'oot movin. Writers usually describe a **character**'s movements while they're speakin. **Check** the extrack from *The Tattie-Bogle* wi a pairtner tae fin oot where the writer has done this.

For example, whit is Erchie daein at the same time as he shouts, 'Speugs!'? Whit is Mrs Erchie daein while she says, 'Ye'd be better wi a tattie-bogle'. Whit effect does this hae? Can ye *see* the characters mair clearly? **Talk** aboot this in the class.

Divide intae groups. **Pick** yin person tae *say* a **sentence**. The rest o the group write it doon. Noo the person daes an action as she/he says the sentence again tae add meanin tae it. The group writes the action doon in words next tae the sentence.

Dae you think the writin is better when ye add action details? Look at the word 'said' in a sentence. Noo change this, addin the action.

mingin stinking

For example, '*Clean up yer bedroom immediately, Mary,*' *said Mum*. We can add a wee extra detail or action that paints a picture o Mum's actions as she talks – jist as the writer has done wi Erchie an Mrs Erchie. '*Clean up yer bedroom immediately, Mary,*' *said Mum, liftin a* **mingin** *cup frae the dressin table.*

Ye can try this wi yer ain imaginative writin but jist for practice **write** five sentences where somebodie is *talkin an makin an action at the same time*.

Changin verbs

Mrs Erchie is 'ruggin up a dandylion.' Whit other verbs could hiv been used here (in Scots or English)?. Is ruggin a good choice? Why?

Fin the following verbs in the passage:

- speired
- scartin
- dichtit
- whurlin
- gallivantin
- quo.

Discuss which other verbs could the writer hiv chosen (in Scots or English)? Pit each o these verbs intae a good sentence.

Addin a life

pages 36-42

As ye've mibbe seen in Chapter 7, a good **short story** makes us believe in the characters. To do this, the writer often gives us lots of **detail** about a character's life. We might learn about their families, their past history, as well as their current circumstances.

The following extract introduces Laurie Forbes, a teenage girl living at home.

Laurie Forbes hid twa jobs. O a mornin, she delivered papers afore schule, syne efter schule she helpit Zoe the hairdresser. She wis a hard wirkin **vratchie**, like her faither afore her. Her faither, Joe, hid bin a fireman...

Joe Forbes hid deed **fechtin** a bleeze on the Dunranald estate, ahin the vandalized shell o the auld scout hut. A bleezin **fag-dowp** drappit bi a druggie...ane o the human tattiebogles that **hirplit** aroon the **roch** grun like **rottens**...hid kinnled a fire amangst the litter. The bleeze **breenged** fae a gairdener's shed. A cannister o gas hid explodit, killin Laurie's faither straicht oot. Daith, an nae divorce, hid brukken the Forbes' hame in twa, leavin the mither alane tae fen fur a **haflin quine** an a bairn nae oot o **hippens**.

Laurie **rowed** her brither in aneth their ma's blankets, an creepit inno the Kitchie tae makk brakfast. Sune, the kettle wis **hotterin**, **caain** muckle runnles o watter tae rin doon the **waas** like giant **greets**.

At seiven in the mornin the Kitchie wis stervin cauld, in a **soss** o hauf-made bairn's bottles an pails o stinkie washin. Mebbe, fin ma's pey came in, they cud speir at Mr Fraser doon the road tae sort their washer. Weet claes, hingin like ghaist's cloots ower a railin, **rikked** afore ae bar o a **teenie** electric fire.

Laurie scraipit a thin **jeelip** o marg ower a **daud** o toast, poored oot twa mugs o coffee, an tuik brakfast **ben** tae her mither. "**Hashed** at the garage?" she speired. Her ma noddit, blearie-eed. "Can I still **gyang** tae Steven's pairty the night?"

From **Leddy-bird, Leddy-bird** by Sheena Blackhall (A Braw Brew, 1997).

See Resources for details

vratchie wretch	**caain** calling
fechtin fighting	**greets** tears
fag-dowp cigarette-end	**waas** walls
hirplit staggered	**soss** muddle
roch rough	**rikked** were hung
rottens rats	**teenie** tiny
breenged burst out	**jeelip** scraping
haflin quine half-grown girl	**daud** hunk
hippens nappies	**ben** through
rowed wrapped	**Hashed** Exhausted
hotterin seething, boiling	**gyang** go

Talking it over

In a group or wi a pairtner hae a **natter** aboot:

1 Whit sort o details has the author gien us aboot Laura as a person? And aboot Laura's family circumstances?

2 How clearly do they help us to imagine Laura's way o life?

3 Can ye identify wi Laura in any way? Mibbe pairts o her life are like yer ain? Mibbe some are gey different?

Scrievin a short story

We've looked at three different weys tae mak folk seem real – addin actions, changin verbs an addin life. Mind yer thochts about thae things an noo **scrieve** a **short story** for *yersel*.

Before startin yer story **invent**, mibbe wi a neighbour, a character like Erchie or Laura *ye're* gan tae write aboot. Decide **who** yer main people are, boy or lassie, man or wimman. Gie them names. Gie them personalities an characters. Dae they girn a lot? Are they happy kinna folk? **Whit** sort o faimilie dae they hiv? **Whaur** is the settin fir the story? Mak it seem real!

STOP!

Now, in groups, **ask** each ither questions aboot the folk ye've invented. By the time yes are finished haein a short discussion, ye should ken yer characters quite weel.

Addin dialogue

Ye might hae noticed that the first extract has a lot of **dialogue** (folk talkin tae each ither) aw the wey through the story, bit the secont extract has mostly **narrative** (naebodie talkin till near the end). Mak shair that ye include some dialogue in *your* story. You decide how much.

Mind an try tae:

1 Add *actions* tae gie a bit mair information aboot a character.

2 Pick *verbs* carefully tae mak yer writing lively an descriptive.

3 Try tae use a least yin *simile* – mair if ye can.

4 Add ither *details* whaur ye can – aboot yer main character an his or he faimilie, aboot their personalities an way o life.

pages 43-46

5 Check back tae aw the ither exercises on story writing. There's lots o help there if ye get stuck wi openins, shapin the story or creatin atmosphere.

pages 67-84

6 Write in Scots, English or a mixture o baith.

If ye're stuck fir an idea tae get startit, ye could model yer story oan the twa above. Either yer main character is ootside in a gairden talkin tae somebodie. An argument taks place. (Set the **scene** then shape your story. What happens in the end? There might be a lot o dialogue in a story like this.) Or ye're in the hoose at hame wi somebodie in yer faimilie. Mibbe, like Laura, ye want tae ask yer folks can ye go tae a pairtie or oot wi a friend. But mibbe ye've a wee brither or sister ye've tae look efter an ye'd raither be somewhere else?

Glossary

Scene
A part of a play AND, from this, an episode in e.g. a comic, short story, novel etc.

13 Short story part one

Starting your story

In the next two chapters of **Turnstones 1** you'll be looking in detail at one short story, **David's Story**. You will examine this story to help you understand how the author approached her writing, and to explore some ideas about how to write a short story: for example, how to handle the characters, themes and motives you'll need to take into account when you're writing your own story. In Chapter 14 you'll be asked to write that short story.

David's Story is © Anne Donovan. It was broadcast by BBC Scotland in Programme 57 of **Talking Points** and audio cassettes are available to schools. The complete story is on the **Turnstones** CD-ROM in Classroom Resources as a copiable, print text.

Background

Sometimes writers just make up a story because an idea comes to them. Sometimes that may happen to you too. But sometimes you'll be asked to write a story on a particular subject, with no control over it, as this writer was.

She was told to write this story for a radio programme for 10 to 12 year olds. The story had to be about 10 minutes long when read out (about 1800-2000 words) and deal with the theme of 'organising support.'

It was part of a number of stories about the same characters. They had all been at primary school together and were starting secondary. The main character is a boy called David who is put in a different class from his friends and feels a bit lonely.

Openings

pages 43-46

You may have already worked through Chapter 8 on Openings. This will be a help because now we're going to look in detail at the different choices a writer can make when opening a story.

As you know, how you start a story is very important since the opening should get the reader's attention and make him or her want to read on.

Now, let's look at two possible openings for the start of **David's Story**.

Opening one

Ma da was makin the dinner when ah walked intae the kitchen.

'How did you get on the day, son?'

'Aw right,' ah said, openin the fridge and takin oot a bottle a ginger.

'Aw right? Yer first day at the secondary – can you no mibbe fill us in wi a wee bit mair detail?'

'Whit d'you want tae know?' Ah sat doon at the table.

'Let's see – where dae ah start? How about, what were the teachers like, what subjects did you get, did you find your way roond the classes OK, did you get any hamework, what were the dinners like, how did yer pals get on? Would that dae fur starters?'

'We didnae really dae that much, da. They kept us in the reggie class for maisty the mornin and we just sat fillin in timetables and that. Then we had wer dinners – it was OK, the chips were rubbish but. In the efternoon we had English and French and we were just gettin wer jotters and books and that. We never done any work.'

'Oh well, ah suppose they'll get you started the morra. How did Joe get on?'

'Aw right, ah think. Never really saw much of him,' ah said.

'How no?'

'He's no in ma reggie class.'

'That's a shame, son. But you can see him at dinner times. Whit aboot Satnam?'

'He's in a different class tae. Ah don't really know anybody in the reggie class.'

'Oh well, you'll soon make new pals. That's what secondary school's like.'

'Aye, right, da. Ah'll away up tae ma room the now.'

'OK, son. Yer tea'll be ready in hauf an hour.'

Opening two

Ah wanted tae be by masel. Didnae want tae talk tae ma da the now. Didnae want tae tell him how rotten it had been. The first day. Ah'd been lookin forward tae it for ages. We all had. Joe came round fur me at eight o'clock this mornin. Ah'd been up since hauf past six. Ma da couldnae believe it. Usually he has tae drag me oot ma bed and there ah wis on that first day; ah'd had ma breakfast, washed ma face, even put on the new school sweatshirt. Aw ready.

We stood in the playground and they called oot wer names and tellt us wer classes. Joe and Cara were in 1B. Kayleigh and Shakeela were in 1E, along with Satnam. One by one everybody ah'd known in primary wis called oot and heided aff tae their class. And when ma name was finally called and ah found masel in this room wi high windaes and bare walls, ah looked round and there wis no even wan person ah recognised. It felt dead strange. Ah mean, ah'm no that shy or that, it's just, well, ah'm no used tae it. And everybody else seemed tae know somebody.

You'll have noticed that **Opening one** is written mainly in **dialogue**. **Opening two** is a **first person narrative**. Make sure you understand what these terms mean before you do the next section.

Examining the openings

If possible, work in groups of four. Two of you should look at **Opening one** and two at **Opening two**.

Read your extract again and **jot** down your answers to the following questions.

- **What** do you learn about David from this extract?

- **What** do you learn about his dad?

- From what he says in the extract, **how** do you think David is feeling about being in a class by himself?

Now get together with the other pair. **Discuss**:

- **What** information do you get from Opening one which is the same as Opening two?

- **What** is different?

And consider this. **Opening one** *and* **Opening two** are *both* in the complete story. What order do you think they should go in? Should **one** come before **two**, or **two** before **one**? Try to give *reasons* for your preference.

 Your teacher may wish each group to report back to the class to compare notes.

Learning about writing

Writers have *choices* about how to tell their story. When you are writing you have a choice too. You have to decide, not just what story you're going to tell but **how** you're going to present it. There isn't necessarily a right or wrong answer to this. Every story is different, every story makes its own rules. But some ways of telling your story will work better for *you and the reader*.

What the writer decided

The writer started with **Opening one**. Her reasons were:

- She felt that the dialogue was a more lively way to start the story.

- She wanted to start with David and his father together because their relationship is important in the story.

- She wanted to show that David was a bit upset about what had happened but didn't want to tell his dad.

- She just liked it better!

Remember, this doesn't mean you were wrong if you preferred it the other way. It's just that, at the end of the day, writers have to decide what they want. When you're the writer, *you* make the decisions.

Considering Voice

Another big decision you need to make (and in some ways the most important one) is the **voice** the story is told in. Two facts are very obvious about this story:

1 It's a **first person** narrative told by David.

2 David speaks in a Scots voice, and is Glaswegian.

Let's look at other ways the writer could have told the story.

Standard English first person version of opening two

I wanted to be by myself. Didn't want to talk to my dad just now. Didn't want to tell him how rotten it had been. The first day. I'd been looking forward to it for ages. We all had. Joe came round for me at eight o'clock this morning. I'd been up since half past six. My dad couldn't believe it. Usually he has to drag me out of my bed and there I was on that first day; I'd had my breakfast, washed my face, even put on the new school sweatshirt. All ready.

Look at the two versions of **Opening two**. Which do you prefer – the Scots version or the standard English version? Can you work out **why**? And again there are no right or wrong answers to this!

Here are two other options – **standard English** and **third person narratives**:

Standard English third person version

David wanted to be by himself. Didn't want to talk to his dad just now. Didn't want to tell him how rotten it had been. The first day. He'd been looking forward to it for ages. Just like all his friends. Joe came round for him at eight o'clock that morning. He'd been up since half past six. His dad couldn't believe it. Usually he had to drag him out of his bed and there he was on that first day; he'd had his breakfast, washed his face, even put on the new school sweatshirt. All ready.

Scots third person version

He wanted tae be by hissel. Didnae want tae talk tae his da the now. Didnae want tae tell him how rotten it had been. The first day. He'd been lookin forward tae it for ages. They all had. Joe came round fur him at eight o'clock that mornin. He'd been up since hauf past six. His da couldnae believe it. Usually he had tae drag him oot his bed and there he wis on that first day; had his breakfast, washed his face, even put on the new school sweatshirt. Aw ready.

Deciding on Voice

You need to think about the best voice to tell the story. If you want to tell a story from *one* person's point of view a *first person narrative* can do that very clearly. Sometimes, though, the story doesn't make sense if only one person tells it – maybe you want to show *different points of view* or perhaps one person couldn't know the whole story. Then a third person voice is needed.

If you choose a first person style it's important to get the voice right. You may want to try out a Scots voice if that's how the character speaks, or you may wish to use another voice which is natural to you. The voice also helps to show the type of person who is speaking.

If you're starting out writing it can help to do a first person narrative in a voice that comes easily to you, so think about how *you* speak yourself.

pages 97-103

You will find more about voice, and about writing in Scots, in the section on plays.

Why the author decided as she did

The author of **David's Story** picked a first person narrative because she felt it gave the story a greater sense of reality and this would help the reader really understand what was happening and what David was feeling and thinking.

She chose the Scots voice because she felt that was how David would speak and it came naturally to her.

With a partner **talk** about the author's decisions .

The author's *options* could be summarised as follows:

Language	Voice
Scots or English	First person or third person

As we've seen, these options lead to four, different stories. Do you think the author was right in her choice? What are the arguments for or against her decision? If she had chosen differently, how would the story have been different? Would you have preferred her to have chosen differently? Why?

On your own, **write** what *you* think down. **Talk** about it in class.

14 Short story part two

Shaping the story

> The plot of a story or a play usually starts off with a character (or characters) in a certain situation. Something then has to happen to create a **crisis** or a **conflict** of some kind. At the start of **David's Story** David goes to secondary school and is put in a different class from his pals. He feels a bit lonely. But if this is all that happened it wouldn't make a story – just a description of how David is feeling. What has to be added?

Something has to happen

Here are some possible ways the story could develop.

1 David could get to know some of the pupils in his new class and become friends with them.

2 David could ask to get moved into the same class as Joe and things would be fine.

3 David could ask his Dad to let him go to another school.

4 David could get abducted by aliens.

5 David could start getting bullied.

In a group or with a partner, try to **decide** which of these *you* think would be the best way to develop the story. What are your reasons for your decision? Discuss your conclusions in class.

Reviewing these options

Probably most of you felt that, while points 1 and 2 make logical sense (and are things that *could* happen in real life), they're not really options for developing the story because they're not very *interesting*. Nothing much would happen and the character wouldn't really develop. We agree.

Point 3 isn't really an option either because it doesn't make sense in terms of the story. Why would David ask his dad to send him to another school? Would he be any happier there? The answer has to be 'No'. This option might fit another kind of story, though.

Some people may have picked point 4 as it seems like the most *exciting* option, but one thing you need to learn about story writing is that excitement is not the only aim! Think of the problem that's been set up. David's not happy because he hasn't got any pals. Being abducted by aliens wouldn't really solve that – again it's an option but for a different kind of story.

But point 5 does seem to make sense. If David is isolated he may well end up being bullied and this means he has a situation he needs to deal with. Also bullying is a common fear of pupils coming to secondary school so it's an *important* theme. Are *you* scared of being bullied? Most of us were, and one of us *was* actually bullied. To be bullied is worrying, but it's not the end of the world!

Developing the plot further

The catalyst

A **catalyst** is something which allows a *reaction* to happen or is something that sets it off. So what is the catalyst for David getting bullied?

Do we need a catalyst? Why couldn't David just get bullied?

The author felt that David wasn't the sort of character who would *automatically* get bullied. He seems like a reasonably confident boy. She also felt that she wanted the hero to be someone the reader could easily identify with – so she could show that bullying might happen to anyone. She was dealing with a real life situation. Does this make sense?

Making choices

Of course, the author had a few choices. There are other ways she could have written it. David's dad could have had an accident, increasing the pressure on the boy. What would have happened then? But it didn't happen in this story! However, this is to let you know that writers have choices and must make decisions. Just keep your conclusions sensible, that's all! So how did **David's Story** develop?

Developing David's Story

A new boy, Eric, arrives in the class and sits beside David. He looks a bit strange and has a lot of problems with his work. Gregsy, the class bully, starts to pick on Eric. David tries to ignore it at first, but then it turns out

that Eric is dyslexic and this is why he is having difficulties. The Learning Support teacher asks David to help Eric by reading out questions to him. Because David is helping Eric, Gregsy starts picking on him.

Why did the author introduce Eric?

Three reasons mainly:

- She felt it made David's character more complex – he is torn between feeling sorry for Eric and wanting to help him, but not wanting to be his friend because he'll get bullied too.

- Dyslexia is a condition a lot of children experience and she wanted it to be mentioned.

- This also helped to develop the idea of 'support' in the story as David has to support Eric. Remember this was the theme that the author had been asked to explore.

Developing the story further

David is now very unhappy. What does he do? *You're* going to pretend to be the author.

Work in a group or pair. Here are a number of possible developments:

1 David asks to be moved to another class.

2 David tells his dad.

3 Eric leaves the school.

4 David does nothing and becomes more and more unhappy.

5 Eric beats up Gregsy.

Look at each of the choices. **Put them in order**, starting with the one you think is *best*. In order to decide, you need to **discuss** *your reasons*. If you can't all agree, let the majority decision carry the day. These choices are not meant to lead to the end of the story, just to the next stage.

What the author decided

She felt that the story was really about David and how *he* felt about the situation. She thought that he wasn't very likely to tell anyone because – remember? – at the beginning of the story he doesn't tell his dad how unhappy he is about being in a different class from his pals. She also felt this was a situation a lot of young people can identify with. It's hard to admit to your parents that you are being bullied and lots of children don't tell. But she did think his dad would ask him. Here is another short extract.

Ma da knew there was sumpn wrang. Wan night he even said, 'Son, is there sumpn wrang? Is somebody bullyin you?'

'Naw da, ah'm OK,' ah said.

'You would tell me if there wis sumpn gaun on, wouldn't you?'

'Aye, da, course ah would. Ah'm fine.'

But ah wisnae fine. And ah started tae hate Eric. Every day he annoyed me mair and mair...

Ending the story

Endings are even more important, in some ways, than beginnings. There's nothing worse coming to the closing part of a story you've been enjoying, and feeling disappointed with the ending.

Some people think a story always has to have a 'twist' in the ending – something unexpected that leaves us shocked or surprised. In fact, this kind of ending is really more suited to horror stories. It's also quite difficult to write. It's best to avoid it in stories which are meant to be like everyday life.

What the author decided

At the first Parents' Night David is at the school with his dad. Eric's mum comes over and tells them both how much David has helped her son. David is surprised as he didn't realise it meant so much to Eric. He tells his dad everything.

So, ah tellt him everythin, includin the stuff aboot Gregsy, and he just nodded.

'But ah don't really know whit she was on aboot, aboot me bein his pal. Ah mean, ah'm no really his pal. Ah just help him wi his readin. Ah don't even like him.'

And ah felt dead rotten even sayin that. Ah mean there wis nothin really wrang wi Eric, he couldnae help the way he looked or that.

'Look son, ah'm no sayin you have tae be Eric's best pal. You don't. But is there any harm in the laddie?'

'Naw dad,' ah said.

'And would you really care aboot folk thinkin you were his pal if it wisnae for this Gregsy?'

'Naw, ah don't think ah would. Ah just wish Joe was in ma class. This wouldnae have happened then. Eric would of sat beside somebody else.'

Ma da smiled. 'David, you might no think you're Eric's pal. But his ma's right – you've been a good friend tae him. You've helped him. And no just wi his readin.'

'Ah suppose so.' Ah'd never thought aboot it afore.

'And talkin aboot pals. Ah thought you and me were pals.'

'Aw, dad.'

'So how come you never tellt me that there wis a problem?'

Ah thought for a moment. Ah didnae really know why ah hadnae tellt ma da, it wis just, ah suppose ah didnae want him tae think there wis sumpn wrang wi me, that the others didnae like me. Ah didnae want him tae think ah wis like Eric. Ah knew it wis daft but ah still couldnae tell him.

'David, if you'd tellt me, mibbe ah could of done sumpn tae help.'

'Dad, whit could you of done? ah said.

'Ah could of come up tae the school, mibbe had a wee word.'

'That wouldnae have done any good,' ah said.

'Mibbe no. But at least ah could of listened tae you. At least you wouldnae have kept it tae yersel.'

Ah looked doon at ma hauns. It wis funny but, just knowin that ma da knew, made me feel better.

'Look, son, see if this ever happens again and you don't tell me ...'

'Ah will.'

'You'd better.'

Why the author ended the story this way

She wanted:

- David's dad to find out what happened but she knew someone else had to tell him.

- to show David growing up a bit and learning something through the incident. Not only does he learn to trust his dad in the future, but he also learns that sometimes you can help someone without realising it.

- an ending that didn't tie up everything neatly. We still don't know what's going to happen about the bullying, for example.

Of course, this is just one person's ideas. You don't need to agree with what the author did. But here's *your* chance to make your own *decisions* – now you're the author!

Writing your own story

You're going to **write** *your* own story about a pupil being bullied after starting secondary school. Before you start, **decide**:

1 the **name** of your character (of course it can be a boy or a girl)

2 the **voice** you're going to write the story in (first or third person, Scots, English, or any other dialect or language)

3 how your story will **develop**. Here are some questions to help you develop your story:

- How does the character feel when he or she is put in a different class from his or her pals?

- Who bullies him or her? What is this person like?

- How does the bullying start? What causes it? (Or does the bully just pick on your character for no reason?)

- How does the character feel?

- Does she or he do anything about the bullying?

- Does he or she tell anyone?

- How does the story develop?

- How does it end?

Alternative writing exercise

If you didn't like the ending of David's Story, you could try writing an *alternative* ending. Take it from the point where David's dad asks him about what's wrong:

Ma da knew there was sumpn wrang. Wan night he even said, 'Son, is there sumpn wrang? Is somebody bullyin you?'

'Naw da, ah'm OK,' ah said.

'You would tell me if there wis sumpn gaun on, wouldn't you?'

'Aye, da, course ah would. Ah'm fine.'

But ah wisnae fine. And ah started tae hate Eric. Every day he annoyed me mair and mair...

Now, what do *you* want to happen? Start writing...

15 Short story part three

The making of atmosphere

Glossary

Relationships
In life how people, and in fiction how characters, behave with one another.

Setting
The place, and its conditions, where the plot happens in a narrative text.

When we read a short story or a novel, watch a film or TV drama, we must be entertained by the events and actions of the story – the plot. We must also feel in touch with the people in the story, the characters, get to know a lot about them, be interested in their relationships and their futures – the **characterisation**. We must also be able to get in on the action with a clear knowledge of where the story is taking place – the atmosphere and the setting. In this section of *Turnstones 1* you're going to look at how to create atmosphere from a different angle to the one you used in Chapter 7.

pages 38-40, 47-50

pages 97-103

Atmosphere is a mix of actions, mood, time, place and the movement of the tale. To create atmosphere you'll need to make the reader see, hear and smell the smells, sights, and sounds of where your story is happening. Often, you'll have to give the taste and feel of things too. How do you do this? Ever worked on a farm? You're going to do so now!

All the following extracts show Andy, a young ploughman, working on a farm. They are taken from **The Wigtown Ploughman** by John McNeillie (G. C. Books Ltd., 1991).

This text is available for DARTs

Using the senses

In this extract Andy is settling into life at the new farm. Here he finishes work for the night and decides that the farmer's wife (the mistress) isn't so bad after all.

He revised his opinion of the mistress when he went in for she said quite pleasantly, 'Andy, boy,' – the 'boy' made her seem more friendly and motherly – 'there's a gles o milk fur ye, an awa tae yer bed, fur ye hae tae get up the morn an ye'll be tired.' He drank the milk in the dark room and removed his boots. The oul man smoked as was his custom. Andy could see him in silhouette against the faint light which came through the window by his chair. The dark head, broad high brow and unruly beard. He sat drawing at his pipe. The daughters were in bed, and Johnnie too had started snoring. The sound of the grandfather clock ticked the minutes away and an ancient cat breathed wheezily under the dresser. Andy went up to bed with the stair creaking under his weight. He smelt Johnnie's earthy clothes, his sweaty socks and the aroma of a hand-rolled cigarette.

In this extract we are given a vivid picture of the inside of the farmer's house at night. **Pick out** the *sounds*, the *sights*, the *smells*, the *tastes* and the sense of *touch* that help to create **atmosphere**.

Working by yourself, **copy** this chart into your jotter (expanded to fit your words) and **fill it in**, having *underlined*, or *highlighted* on your photocopy, the words or phrases you think are best.

Sounds	Sights	Smells	Tastes	Touch

Were any senses not described in this extract? For example, we're not told how the milk tasted to Andy. Add a sentence to this extract on your photocopied sheet which might describe the taste. Write sentences which will add other important details about Andy's experience in the farmhouse.

Looking at actions

This time we see Andy at the end of a working day.

A great watery blister rose on his thumb, but he raked on it till it burst and then sucked it to ease the pain.

Three blasts on the whistle told them it was 'drappin tim'. Andy felt that for him it was just about as near dropping time as he would ever be. He sat down at once and undid his boots to tip the hay seeds from them, taking off stockings too, to clean the powder and dust from his feet. The reaper became silent and soon Johnnie came leading the horses across the field. Once again Andy rode the black mare to the stable, helped to remove the sweat-drenched harness, and roll the lines. While the horses were feeding he called the dog, Spot, and went for the kye. Johnnie washed himself and went for his porridge. The dog did the running and Andy shouted and threw stones to hurry the kye up the road to the byre. The three women came out to chain them and he went in to the house. Johnnie was on his way to the byre with a sack apron round his waist and his sleeves rolled high.

The oul man was sittin by the fire smoking, for every farmhouse in that country had a fire all the year round.

'They tell me ye wur workin hard this efternin, boy,' he said, 'weel, ye'll hae din the day whun ye hae milked yer kye. It'll no be sae sair on ye the morn.'

Andy supped his porridge in silence and rose to go to the byre. The byre was filled with the sound of chewing kye and milk spurting into pails; the sweat and hair of the cow he was milking stuck to his arms and neck. The chains jingled; the kye were let out; the dog barked them down to the field; he emptied his pail and rubbed the hairs from his skin before going in for his supper.

The writer has chosen his words very carefully, painting a clear picture for us by showing the many actions taking place. This all helps to create the atmosphere of farm life.

Make a list of the *actions* that take place. Each might start like this:

● Andy raked...
● Andy sucked his thumb...
● The whistle blew...

 But make up *your* own.

Looking at Andy

The last extract from **The Wigtown Ploughman** shows Andy in the middle of many different jobs.

When the last of the kye had been chased down the byre to prevent them soiling the walk, and the gate of the field had been shut upon them, the oul man of the field came to watch Andy clean the byre. The barrow was large and heavy; its sides and wheel were caked with dung so that it was difficult for him to wheel it empty. He pushed the long-handled brush and cleaned the walk; carried pails of water and brushed till his face was as red as Johnnie's. He shovelled and swept, and, when the barrow was almost full, he wheeled it, staggering along the slippery plank to tip it on the midden.

The road had to be swept too, and afterwards the pigs had to be fed. It was wearying work, and at half-past nine, as he walked round the pig-houses with arms straining under the weight of the pails of mash, he wished for noon, but the morning wore on with the feeding of hens, sweeping the stable, washing milk-pails, carrying water, and washing the dairy floor.

Not only are Andy's actions described, we also learn about the tools and implements used on the farm. We get a strong sense of activity and of Andy himself. He must have been exhausted at the end of all this hard work!

- **Make a list** of the *words* used to describe how tired Andy is. To do this look at the sort of words the writer uses, especially those describing actions – the **verb**s. List any other words that add to this effect. (If you have a photocopied sheet, underline these words.)

- What other methods does the writer use to tell us how hard-worked Andy is? You might, as a wee example, consider the way he adds details, one after another.

STOP!
- Do we get to see into Andy's thoughts?

Putting it together

The recipe

pages 43-46

Again **write** the opening – or maybe the whole – of a short story. Create a very clear sense of place and a strong sense of atmosphere. Make it about work – *hard* work. Use some of the techniques you've just studied.

- Pick somewhere you know well. Invent a character to put into this place. It might even be yourself! Perhaps you've worked *really* hard somewhere too? If you've never worked hard in your life, you're lucky. So, as a wee punishment for your idleness, you'll just have to imagine it...

- Try to pick a place with lots of smells and sounds. As you write keep asking yourself, What can I hear? see? taste? smell? touch?

- Decide on the time of year, time of day, weather – all the ingredients you can think of that help create a strong description of where the story is taking place.

These details will make your story's atmosphere.

Here are some places we can think of where hard work takes place:

- Kitchen.

- Baker's shop.

- Café and restaurant.

- Sports stadium.

- An ice-rink.

See Visual Workpoint V8, V12

- Your own or someone else's house.

- A sweatshop in a foreign country.

- A market-place.

pages 51-54

And remember, if you are going to write a whole short story, you'll need to think about **image**ry, plot and characterisation as well. Another job!

16 Poetry

Poems from pictures

What sort of **poems** do you enjoy most? Which ones do you write?
About yourself, and what is happening in your life? About an
incident? About a memory? Or do you write ballads where you tell
a story? Writing poetry lets you explore events and feelings, and a
bundle of old poems can work in much the same way as a diary –
memories written down.

Subjects for poems

There are so many subjects we can write about. We can write about
ourselves, or about other people, or places we have seen, and sometimes a
painting can be a good inspiration for a poem.

We're now going to use paintings by a weel kent (*well known*) painter called
Joan Eardley. She lived between 1921 and 1963 in Scotland and
England. She painted pictures of city life with town buildings and city
children. She also painted beautiful country scenes of landscapes, fields of
hay, farm animals and workers, the sea, at different times of day and night,
and in different weathers.

Here are three poems beside the paintings which inspired them.

They're from **The Sweetie Poke** (Markings Special Edition, 1999,
ISBN 1 901913 19 7), a collection of poetry by school pupils based on
Joan Eardley paintings.

The Evacuees

The war has started
ma ma has sent us away
it's freeezin I'm shiverin
ma brither's got the cal
I'm gled ma brither's here

we've got oor claes in oor bags
we're gan far away
we come fae Glesga
we're gan tae Girvan tae save us fae the bombs
I'm gled ma brither's here

we're waiting at Central Station
tae get the train tae Girvan
tae get us safe fae the Nazis
I'm gled ma brither's here

Oh no the snow has started
I'm freezin I've only got ma skirt on
I'm gled ma brither's here

hurry up train
hurry up we're freezin and starvin
we want tae get tae a safe place
I'm gled ma brither's here

hurry up train
hurry up train
I'm gled ma brither's here

I wonder what the hoose is like
I wonder if the people are nice
I wonder if there's lots of kids
I wonder
I wonder
I wonder
I'm gled ma brither's here

By Eileen Walker **of** Park Primary School, Stranraer

The Khaki Shirt

Is he walking out of the war with dirt on his face?
Is he walking out of the war slowly on purpose
thinking of the people who died?
Is he walking out of the war quickly because an
airstrike is going to come?
But he always wore his khaki shirt.

Are you an old fashioned model walking down the
aisle with new clothes on?
Are you an old fashioned model thinking how cold
you'll be once this is all over?
Are you an old fashioned model wearing horrible
trousers?
But he always wore his khaki shirt.

He's gone into the army thinking 'I'll be dead at the
end of this'.
He's gone into the army, he's made a lot of tears
come down.
He's gone into the army fighting for his country.
But he always wore his khaki shirt.

By **Emma Hughes** of Rephad Primary School

waterfall: joan eardley

water is falling
a grey mare's tail
        tumbling

thin
stream
of
grey and white
in the green hill

one rush of brown spray tells
there's a peat bog lurking
relic from centuries past

'come hail or high water'
as the saying goes
the waterfall will fall
will fall
but sure as the tide shifts
our ashes will mix with peat
or catch in a frolic of foam

just the sound of a peewit's song stays
or a far lamb's new call
and the water falling

    water falling

falling

By **Liz Niven**

Discussion

The poets have thought about the **content** of their poems, the *form* of
their poems as well as the **voice** they choose to write in. Let's think about
this before we write our own poems. **Talk** together about the following
matters, either in class or in small groups.

Content

With a partner, read the three poems very carefully – aloud if you can. What are they telling us? This is the **content**, what the poem is about. For example, in **waterfall** the poet has started her poem with a description of the picture, the colours and shape of the waterfall. Poems often *seem* to be about one thing but are *actually* about something important that the poet might want to say.

Is this poem just about the waterfall? What else is the poet talking about? When does she move away from describing the waterfall into other matters?

In **The Khaki Shirt**, although the poem describes the boy in great detail, the pupil has used a special way of writing about him. What has she done?

Form

Form is a complicated word. Here it means the *shape* or *organisation* of a poem, or anything that appears on a page – a bit like **lay-out**.

Ask yourselves some, or all, of these questions and search for answers.

- **Look** at the way the poems are *arranged* on the page. What does **waterfall** remind you of? Is there a pattern of some kind in any of the poems?

- **Check** the number of **verses**. How many have been used? What shape do they take? Do different things happen in each verse?

- Are they rhyming poems? Do they have **rhythms** instead? Why do you think there are no capital letters in **waterfall**?

- Could you think about **content** and **form** when you write your poems?

Glossary

Verse
Lines in a poem that form an obvious group on the page.

 STOP!

Now, write your own poem

Choose a picture, a painting or a photograph you would like to write about. Have it by you as you write. *Don't choose* it just because you like it *vaguely*. *Choose it* because it makes you feel *strongly* in some way or another. Does it make you feel sad? Fearful? Angry? Peaceful? Sorry for the person in the picture? Wish you were there? Curious about the artist or photographer and what he or she was thinking?

Here's a way to set about writing your poem.

1 Write down the name of the picture. If it doesn't have one, give it a name – four words at most. This is your title (for the moment).

2 Choose two or three sentences to describe the painting or photograph.

3 Now decide whose **voice** will speak in the poem. Sometimes the poet pretends to be someone else. For example, who is speaking in **Evacuees**?

4 For your poem you might choose from these subjects:

- The person who painted the picture or took the photograph – what was the artist thinking as she or he worked? Why did the artist choose this subject? How did he or she feel painting or photographing this subject?

- You might just describe what you are looking at.

- You are a person or thing in the picture. You are the peewit, the water, the soldier in the khaki shirt, the wee girl or boy being evacuated. If so, what are you thinking? How do you feel?

- You might ask the people in the picture questions about themselves – *Why are you looking so sad? What's happened to you?* (**Hint**: Look at **The Khaki Shirt**. The characters might talk to you!)

- You might like to be in this picture yourself. You might imagine lying in the sun by a burn (imagine one you know well, it could help) listening to the bird sounds.

- You might try to imagine being involved in a war where you must leave home and the poem explains how you might feel.

 Once you have decided on the **voice** of your poem, **write** *your* poem in that voice. You have just written a first draft of your poem.

Review your poem

- Did you try to use unusual **images** or **phrases** to describe anything?

- Have you divided your poem into **verses**? If so, something slightly different should be happening in each verse. You could give a new piece of information or perhaps a new person speaks.

 - What sort of ending did you find? Apart from descriptive lines, are there any emotions or feelings to end the poem?

'Tricks' to use in poems

Can we add anything to make your poem *even better*? Ask your poem the following questions.

- Do you have any lines where more *description* could be added? Extra details? Do you 'fit' with the picture? (Look again at it.)

- Do you need to *rhyme* more *or* less? (Sometimes it's very difficult to find rhyming words and sometimes a word might get chosen not because it's the best word, but just because it rhymes.)

- Instead, would you like *patterns* and *rhythms?*

- Do you have a repeated line to give a *pattern?* (Look again at **The Evacuees** and **The Khaki Shirt**)

- Would you like me to repeat the *title* of the poem? (Saying it aloud will let you hear the rhythm. This line could start or end your poem. It might appear at the end or start of each verse.)

- Would a **simile** or a **metaphor** – or two, or more – help you? (For example, try comparing one thing in the picture with something else.)

- Or perhaps some **alliteration**? (This would sometimes mean repeating the same sound several times. The last sentence we used just did it with the sound 's'. Or, think about the 'The **c**ool, **kh**aki shirt'.)

Now check through your poem and see if you could *improve* it by using any of the above 'tricks'. **Redraft** your poem if necessary, adding more touches depending on how your poem has answered the questions above.

Next, **exchange** your poem with a neighbour and let him or her read it while you read theirs. Ask each other questions about your poems. You might find this helps you to make even more corrections and add more detail.

Now read your poems aloud in class, and/or put them on the wall. Enjoy the sounds and images you have all created.

You might try this exercise with other artists or photographers whose work you like. Even better, go to an **Art Gallery** and write from real paintings, sculptures or photographs!

Writing in Scots

You might want to write your poem in Scots. For example, 'Little Girl with a Squint' could become 'Wee Lassie wi a Squint'.

Mind ye can use Scots an English thegither in yer poems. Just write it the way you would say it. That's the best guide. If you're writing in Scots don't worry too much about the spelling just now. Concentrate on how your poem will *sound.*

Glossary

Alliteration
Using and repeating the same letter or sound in a phrase or sentence.

Redraft
A piece of writing rewritten after editing (also used as a verb).

See the Visual Files for interesting images

17 Plays and scripts part one

The basics

Plays, and **scripts**, are different from most other types of writing because they are meant to be *performed*, not simply read silently to oneself. Here, we'll concentrate on plays written for the stage, though you can also write scripts for radio, television or films. Although scripts are written in much the same way as plays, they are different from each other. But we'll ignore the differences for the moment.

Structure and lay-out

Let's look first at the structure of plays and how they look on the page – the **lay-out**.

Structure

Plays are usually divided into **acts** and **scene**s. An act is a big section of a play, usually taking around half an hour to perform, though times can vary. Long plays often have three, or maybe even five, acts. Short plays are sometimes not divided into acts and for that reason such a play is sometimes described as a *one-act play*.

Acts are usually divided into **scenes**. A new scene usually takes place when there is a change of place or time. At the start of the scene you write the place it is happening, and sometimes the time. Normally you say which characters are in that scene – the names typed sometimes in **bold**, sometimes in capital letters. For example

> **Scene 4**. The Moon. Early morning.
>
> (**LITTLE MO** and **BIG HETTY**)

You might also find some description of the stage set at the start of a scene. In printed texts this is usually set in **italic**s, and in brackets. For example:

> *(We are on some kind of lunar base, with boxes of technology here and there. Screens are flashing information we cannot read. Through a window we half-glimpse a black sky and jagged mountains. The stage is nearly hidden by washing lines and hanging laundry. At first we don't see Little Mo and Big Hetty. We can only hear them.)*

Lay-out

A first glance at how a play or script is set on the page makes it obvious that the lay-out is completely different from what you'd find in a novel or an essay. The lay-out of a play is important as it shows the actors, the director and the set-designer what the *writer intends*.

When you read different plays you will see slight variations in how the writers (or their publishers) use lay-out. The most important thing is that it is clear and looks the same all the way through the script.

Bill's New Frock by Anne Fine (BBC/Longman, 1990) gives us a good example of how to set out a script clearly.

Glossary

Bold
A form of type with **darkened** lettering used to emphasise words (see italic).

Glossary

Italic
Form of type with *lightened* lettering sloping to the right, used for emphasis or to show quotation (see **bold**).

In this extract, the main character a boy, Bill, wakes up one morning to discover he has a serious problem…

Scene 1: Bill's bedroom

(BILL, MUM, DAD and BELLA, the cat)

(*An alarm clock rings.*)

BILL When I woke up this morning, something really strange had happened. Oh, my room looked exactly the same. And all the stuff in it looked exactly the same. Even the mirror looked exactly the same. But when I looked in the mirror, I didn't look exactly the same at all. I'd turned into a girl!

I don't believe this! Is it a *dream*? Is it a *nightmare*? What is going on?

MUM (*calling*) Bill! Bill! hurry up! Time to get dressed for school!

BILL This can't be true. This can't be happening. I must still be asleep.

MUM (*coming in*) Oh, good. You're awake.

BILL That's it, then. I'm not asleep.

MUM Up you get. Time to get dressed. Why don't you wear this pretty pink frock?

BILL Don't drop that frock over my head! Mum, don't! Stop it! I can't breathe. (*gurgle, gurgle*) Mu-um!

MUM There. Now it's on. I'll leave you to do up all the pretty little shell buttons. I'm late for work.

BILL This can't be true. This simply cannot be true. Where's Dad? He'll sort me out. Dad! Dad!

DAD Well, hello, poppet! You look very sweet today. It's not often we see you in a frock, is it?

BILL Dad -

DAD Take care now. I'm late for work.

BELLA Miaowwwww. Miaowwwww.

BILL Hello, Bella. At least you don't notice any difference in me, do you? I look the same to you. Oh, Bella! Is this a dream? Or a nightmare? Do I have to go to school like this?

BELLA Miaowwwww.

BILL Yes. I suppose I do…

Laying your play out clearly

Make sure you deal with these two questions.

- **Who** is speaking?
  The name of the character who is speaking is in CAPITAL LETTERS at the left-hand side of the page so it is clear *who* is speaking. Always leave a space between the name of the character and her or his speech. If you are hand-writing, not word-processing the play, you should put the name in the margin with a colon (:) after it.

- **What** are the stage directions?
  Stage directions are the words the actors don't say! When you want to tell an actor to do something (for example, to leave the 'room', or to take off her coat) you put the directions, the words, in brackets. For example, (*leaves the room*), (*taking off her coat*). If you're using a word-processor set the stage directions in *italics*, as we're doing here.

- Occasionally, you need to tell the actor how to say a particular line, (for example, *angrily*, *nervously*) and this should be in brackets too. You don't need to do this a lot – usually it should be obvious from your words how a line needs to be said, or else the director decides.

Making it sound real

Just because the words are set out correctly doesn't necessarily mean it's a good play. It has to *sound real* when it is performed. Let's look at some of the ways a writer makes a play *sound* as if it should be spoken, rather than read silently.

Informal language

Glossary

Formal
Following set rules.

Most of the time, especially at home or with people we know well, our spoken language is less **formal** than our written language. We often use shortened versions of words (*don't* instead of *do not*, for example) and we rarely speak in complete sentences.

For most of the time in a play or script the characters speak **informal**ly, unless they are in a situation which requires them to take a different approach to their language. **What** might that situation be? (Some suggestions follow.)

Saying it

Things to do

In a small group of four, read out the extract from *Bill's New Frock*. Each of you takes one of the four parts. Now look again at the script and make a note in your jotter of any words or phrases which you think are examples of **informal** language.

Of course, sometimes in a play, just as in real life, people *do* use *formal language* when they are speaking. If you were writing a scene in a courtroom or wanted to show a Head Teacher giving a talk to an assembly, you would need to use formal language.

With your partner, find other examples of places **where** people speak in a formal way. Think of work places where people wear suits, and, if they're men, collars and ties, or maybe uniforms with lots of gold on them. List ten or so examples.

Then, talk about something that interests you both. That's easy, isn't it? But this is the difficult bit (and using a tape recorder or a videorecorder for this exercise would make it a lot easier) *really* **listen** to the language you're using. Answer these four questions.

1 Were you talking informally, or formally?

2 Were you talking in **sentences**?

3 What sorts of **punctuation** were you using?

4 How clearly were the **word**s you used separated from one another?

Having done that, **discuss** between yourselves in what ways writing is different from talking, and why this should be so. **Note** your ideas down, and **talk** about them in class.

Glossary

Punctuation
Marks used in writing to show such things as pauses, sentences and how to say words, e.g. commas, full stops and exclamation marks.

18 Plays and scripts part two

The words and the writing

In the previous chapter we looked at lay-out. We also began talking about the language used in plays and scripts – how we *actually* talk together for most of the time. This language is different from the language we use when we are in formal situations. It is also different from the language we find in most of the materials we read and write. We're going to continue discussing the matter of spoken language and Scots. We're also going to ask you to write a play or script.

Glossary

Dialect (also called a *variety*)
A language obviously different from other, related languages in its words, how they are used, and in its accent or words and their use, e.g. Geordie, Doric, standard English, **Bajan** etc.

Bajan is the dialect of English spoken in Barbados in the West Indies. Each part of the world where English is spoken has its own distinctive dialect. *All* dialects serve the purposes of their communities and are of equal worth.

Words and place

People who live in the same place don't all speak exactly the same – there are different **accent**s, **dialect**s and languages used in Scotland. Using these different forms of **voice** in a play is a good way of bringing speeches to life.

There are various ways you can do this and we're now going to look at a few of them.

The following extract is from a play called **Space Invaders** by Alan Spence (Hodder and Stoughton, 1994). It is set in a Scottish town in the present day. The play centres round a man called Andrew who has seen a UFO (an unidentified flying object). Lynn is Andrew's 16-year-old daughter. In this extract she meets Doug, who has been studying UFOs for some time. Doug is sitting on a hill.

DOUG It's brilliant up here. No kidding. It's magic. See on a clear day? I bet you...I bet if you looked out to the west there you can see the Empire State Building! (*looks up*) I wish they'd hurry up and come back. (*calls out*) Hello! I'm here! I'm waiting! How is it a wee guy like Andy there, no even interested in UFOs, couldn't care less about them, and they come to him. I mean no harm to the guy, but he is just ordinary. Normal even. Straight. Know what I mean? And here's me. (*shrugs*) Maybe if I concentrate really hard. Focus my energies. Open up the channels.

(*Sits cross-legged, eyes closed, breathes deep.*)

Enter **LYNN**. She doesn't see **DOUG**. He opens his eyes.

DOUG Hey! (*she jumps*)

LYNN Och, it's you.

DOUG Not at school today?

LYNN Does it look like it?

DOUG You're really far out!

LYNN Give us a break, will you? Far out!

DOUG No, really. I like all that punk stuff. It's great.

LYNN I'm *not* a punk. Punk's dead years ago.

DOUG Helluva sorry. What are you then?

LYNN I'm just *me*.

DOUG Right!

LYNN And I don't like hippies.

DOUG That's no very nice, is it?

LYNN Who wants to be nice?

DOUG It's nice to be nice.

LYNN Don't *say* that.

DOUG Why not?

LYNN It's the kind of thing my ma and da say. Specially when they've got a drink in them. 'Ach aye. Nice to be nice. Know what I mean.'

DOUG Nothing wrong wi that.

Saying it

Read the extract out loud with a partner, each of you playing a part. If you didn't know it was set in Scotland, which words and phrases do you think would tell you? Make a note of them.

Space Invaders suggests the place its characters are in, the **setting**, by using Scots words. But there are many different versions of Scots. Look at this extract from a play called **It's A Braw Brew** by Ann Matheson (from **A Braw Brew**, Watergaw, 1997).

Cast: MITHER, FAITHER, GRANNIE, BRIAN AN FIONA, GENIE.

Set: *Kitchen, wi mither settin table an grannie in chair knittin.*

MITHER (*Lookin at watch*) Gie thae weans a shout, mither. Their tea's near ready. Tam's workin late the night so he'll no be hame.

Grannie goes tae windae.

GRANNIE Brian! Fiona! Yer tea's ready. (*Goes to table*) Whit are we haein the nicht, Isa? It smells awfy guid. Mince an tatties?

MITHER Naw, spaghetti bolognaise.

GRANNIE Och ye ken hou Ah hate yon foreign muck. Ah'd hae been better bidin at hame an haein twa byelt eggs.

Fiona an **Brian** rush in.

BRIAN Mither, see whit we fun at the cowp.

MITHER Whit were ye daein at the cowp? Hou aften dae Ah hae tae tell ye tae stey away frae there? Ye dinna ken whit ye cud catch.

BRIAN But luik at this mither. (*He produces a dirty Irn-Bru bottle that has a strange glow.*) Whit d'ye think o that, eh?

Saying it

pages 62-65

In a group of three, **read** the extract *out loud*, each member playing a part. Take note of any Scots word which is new to you. Find out its meaning from the group, your classmates, teacher, family or a good Scots dictionary.

In this small group, look again at the extracts from **Space Invaders** and **It's A Braw Brew**. Which of them is nearer to the version of Scots which is spoken in your family or local area? What are the resemblances, what is quite different? Why do you think this is?

See **Scotland's languages** and/or **Scots for bairns**

Making choices about writing in Scots

If you choose to write some or all of a script in a version of Scots, you need to decide which words to use. Alan Spence in **Space Invaders** suggests that the play is set in Scotland by using a few Scots words while Ann Matheson in **It's A Braw Brew** makes it much more obvious.

Here are some words you could use:

- *Ah* (or *ah*) instead of I
- *the day* instead of *today*
- *ma* instead of *my*
- *scunnered* instead of *fed up*, and so on.

Sometimes there are a number of different words for the same thing or person, e.g. *mither, ma, mammy, maw, mum*.

Putting it in writing

Here are some exercises to help you think about **word** choice on your own or with a partner. You may choose one or your teacher may suggest one.

- **Rewrite** the **Space Invaders** extract to make it into a broader form of Scots, or one which you know better.

- **Rewrite** the **It's A Braw Brew** extract in a form of Scots which is more familiar to you

- **Rewrite** either extract in a dialect which is more familiar to you, including **standard English**.

Showing a character's feelings through word choice

As well as suggesting where the character comes from, the choice of words and the way they are arranged into sentences show what the character is like and how he or she is feeling. Look at another section from **Space Invaders**.

In this section Andrew, who thinks he has seen a UFO, is being interviewed on local radio by a DJ called Jimmy.

JIMMY   So tell us about it, Andrew.

ANDREW   (*awkward*) Well I was up the community centre like.

JIMMY   Uh huh.

ANDREW   And I went for a walk up the Law.

JIMMY   That's the hill up the back there?

ANDREW   That's right. Yes.

JIMMY   And what happened?

ANDREW   Well, it's all woods up there. And I was just walking along, quite the thing, minding my own business. And the first thing I noticed was a buzzing noise. And there was this funny smell.

JIMMY   What kind of smell?

ANDREW   Sort of...metallic.

JIMMY   Uh huh.

ANDREW   Then I came round into this clearing and there it was sitting there.

JIMMY   What was it?

ANDREW   Just like a big ball of light, you know. Really bright.

JIMMY   So how did you feel?

ANDREW   Scared.

The stage direction tells us that Andrew is awkward. But it's not just the stage direction. In a small group, or with a partner, pick out any words or phrases which show you that Andrew is feeling awkward and unsure of himself.

Putting it in writing

By yourself, **rewrite** this extract, *changing* it so that Andrew comes across as a confident, talkative man who is desperate to tell his story to Jimmy.

Action! Action! Action!

The characters are important but drama is basically about action.   In a play – and most other forms of writing – you have to keep the action moving.   You don't want the characters to spend too much time talking about things which are not at the centre of the story, the **narrative**.

Look back at the extract from **It's A Braw Brew**. The writer spends a few moments at the beginning of the play showing us what grannie and mither are like (grannie complaining about the food, mither busy getting the tea ready) but as soon as Brian and Fiona come home they produce the bottle that is going to be the main focus for the action of the play (Why? Because there's a genie inside it!). If the writer had kept on with the conversation between grannie and mither for another page, or if, when Brian and Fiona came in, we had another page about why they were late, the audience might get bored.

Try to remember this when you are writing your own play.   So why wait? Let's get started!

Writing a play

You may have your own ideas for a play or you could try one of these suggestions, either on your own, with a partner or in a small group. Your teacher will decide. If you're writing with others you'll have to *agree* on four important matters:

- the details of the **plot**
- the **language**
- the nature of the **characters** – **who** they are and the sorts of people they are
- **where** the action is to take place.

There should also be a part for *everybody* in your group in the play.

Play One

The plot: A pupil has lost an expensive item (for example, a mobile phone, personal stereo, jewellery, watch). It is discovered in the bag of another pupil in the class. This pupil gets blamed for stealing it but he or she knows he or she didn't do it.

You could write one or all of the following scenes:

1 The pupil realises the item is missing.
2 The item is discovered in the other pupil's bag.
3 The head teacher interviews the 'thief'.
4 The 'thief' tells his or her parents what happened.
5 The real thief is discovered.

Play two

The plot: A boy or girl (you choose) has moved house and starts secondary school four weeks into the term. He or she doesn't know anyone. The pupil is introduced to the class by the teacher who asks another pupil to look after her or him. Write a short play based on what you think might happen.

Act *your* plays in front of the class, or in your Drama class. Videotaping or audiotaping them will allow you to talk about the plays, and the performances – and to have a good laugh.

See Visual Workpoints V10

In between the laughs, **discuss** the improvements that might make your plays better.

19 Persuasion part one

Advertising

> People try to **persuade** you to do things all the time. They try to make you behave as *they* want you to behave. *Do this. Don't do that. Buy this. Think like me.* Persuasion is found everywhere. We're doing it in this book! Sometimes it's accompanied by reasons, explanations. Sometimes it may even be accompanied by a *please*! Most times it's not. Sometimes the persuasion is helpful – we think ours is – but when you're being persuaded you should be thinking about the *process*, asking yourself questions...what sorts of questions? About what? *Please*, read on.

About persuasion

Persuasion, or attempts to persuade, are commonplace in Scotland, and around the world. If you're reading a newspaper, watching TV or listening to radio, for example, people will be trying to persuade you to do something at least 10 or 20 times an hour – probably much more often. So **who** is doing the persuading? Would you believe *millions* of people? Think about it. Here are a few examples.

- DJs try to *persuade* you to like the record they're playing and maybe even to buy it. (Of course, they don't say this openly, but few people in the business of persuasion ever reveal their intentions. Have *we?*)

- Head teachers try to *persuade* you to wear school uniform.

- Teachers try to *persuade* you to choose their subjects. (Except English, of course. It's so good it's compulsory – you have to do it!)

- Your mum and dad (and *every* mum and dad) try to *persuade* you to go to bed at a reasonable time on a school night.

There are also many ways **how** people persuade other people to do things. And **remember**, just because you **agree** with the ideas and opinions being given to you does not mean you're not being persuaded! Here are some of the methods that people might use to persuade you:

- **Leaflets** dropped in at the front door – from businesses like local restaurants, supermarkets or DIY shops – *eat here, shop with us.*

pages 116-120

- **Through talking and speaking** – sometimes this can be on a special occasion, like a **debate**, or in a day-to-day situation like an argument between friends. Usually it will be about persuading someone, or a group, to share one point of view.

- **Famous people on TV**, or **articles**, **letters** and **editorials in newspapers** – all of them expressing opinions on some topic, all of them trying to persuade the audience to see the truth of a particular belief.

- Party political broadcasts – politicians persuade you to vote for them (if you are old enough).

- Persuasion from pressure groups (e.g. Greenpeace, anti-nuclear movements, etc.) – to support their cause.

In all these different ways, and there are hundreds of others, people and organisations try to persuade you to do what *they* want and to see things the way *they* do. You've probably often tried – or wanted – to *persuade* some members of the human race to do something your way!

One of the most powerful and common ways of persuading us to do things – that is, **to buy things** and **to spend money** often – is **advertising!**

Glossary

Argument
A discussion to support or oppose an idea.
Audience
The person or persons reading, watching or listening to a text (see target audience).

Advertising

Advertising

Once advertising was done by the town crier. Now most advertisements are carried by mass media. The usual intention of advertising is persuasion – to buy a product, or to accept an idea, sometimes both. Advertising is a multi-million pound business and meets the costs, for example, of radio and television programmes, and reduces the price of newspapers and magazines. Advertising is widespread and it works. We're *all* affected by it.

Mass media

Mass media are sometimes persuasive, trying to make us behave in a certain kind of way; sometimes they give us information; sometimes they are entertaining; sometimes all three together. Forms of mass media that are printed are called **print media**. Photographs, television, film and special effects (SFX), for example, are called **visual media**. Nowadays, print and visual media are mixed together on our screens, usually accompanied by **sound media** like background music, pop music, dialogue, and sound effects.

Advertisements (ads as they're commonly called) always try to sell us things, usually products or ideas. But they can also be used to **promote interest** in issues (for example, the environment) and **raise awareness** of causes (for example, banning fox-hunting, saving the planet from global warming).

All sorts of people want us to buy things, products and ideas, all the time. They usually hire **advertising agencies** to help them. These are businesses that specialise in making ads.

Thinking about ads

page 10

Before we tell you about some of the important things you need to know about advertising, take a look at the ad below. Try to **work out** how it works! Remember the keys on reading? They will be of help to you.

Answering the following questions will also help you to organise your ideas. Do this *on your own*.

1   **What** is the ad trying to sell or promote? (In other words, what is it trying to persuade us to buy? **Hint**: this may be more than the product!)

2   **How** does It try to sell the product to us? (How does it *try to* persuade us to buy?)

3   **Who** is the ad aimed at, who is the **target audience**? (A particular age group? A certain sort of person? Who?)

4   In **what** kind of *print mass media* might you expect to find this kind of ad? Give an example of **where** you might find it? Where you would *not* find it?

5   Would you be *persuaded* to buy the product? Why?

First, **write** down *your* ideas about these questions. Then **discuss** your ideas with a partner and compare notes. **Write** down your findings.

After you have had some time to talk about them, your teacher will ask you for feedback, either in a larger group or in the whole class. You should **decide** on the *main ideas* you want to put into that response and who will announce them to the whole class.

Talking it over

How successful were you in *persuading* the rest of the class to take *your* ideas on board?

What was the best idea? The craziest, the one that made you laugh?

What ideas about ads did most of the class seem to have? Where do you think these ideas come from? **Who** did the persuading? **When**? **Why**? If everybody, or most, people in the class all have these ideas, is this an example of *really* successful persuasion?

 See **Resources**.

20 Persuasion part two

The advertising agency

Big, expensive advertisements are made by **advertising agencies**. The sort that appear in newspapers and magazines are sometimes called **display advertisements**. The smaller kind your mum or dad might put into a newspaper to sell something – a bike or a washing machine, for example – are called **classified advertisements**.

Your task

Work in groups of five or six. Each group is now going to pretend to be a team working in an agency making a print medium *display advertisement*. One of you will be in charge of advertising. That person is the Marketing Director. *Every person in the group will take the Director's orders without question.*

First, the group (or your teacher) appoints the Marketing Director. Then, together, give your advertising agency a name. The Director will decide. See the resources panel for examples of three different sorts of name (and the work that the agencies with these names really do).

Glossary

Search engine
Programs on the Internet allowing users to search for files and information.

Browser
Computer program for reading and moving between texts on the Web.

Resources

If you want to find out more about advertising agencies visit one or more of the following Websites.

The Union
www.union.co.uk/
Award-winning Scottish advertising agency. The site provides information on its services and clients, plus examples of its work.

WKL Advertising & Design
www.wkl.co.uk/
Advertising agency offering multimedia and traditional design. Site includes staff profiles, contact details and a portfolio of work.

McCann-Erickson UK
www.mccann.co.uk/
Leading international advertising agency. Site provides details on the organisation's integrated disciplines, success stories, and facts and figures.

There are many others. Put 'Advertising Agencies' into your search engine and use your browser to find out just how many!

Test marketing is when a product is put on sale in a region to test what buyers think of the product and the sales techniques associated with it. If successful, it will then be marketed nationally, usually with modifications.

You are now about to create an advertisement for a **client** – the owner of the product to be advertised. (The client will be played by your teacher.)

The client, Kandy Korporation, wants your group to design a *half-page, colour advertisement* for **The Daily Record** (and, possibly, other national mass media) for a new product targeted on young people aged between 10 and 25. Other groups in the agency are handling ads for other mass media. The product is being **test-marketed** in Central Scotland before being put on the UK and European market.

Your product

It is a biscuit made of two, thick ice cream wafers on the outside containing a core of soft, raspberry ice cream. Each wafer is covered on its inner side with a thin layer of gooey caramel. The whole biscuit is robed (covered) in milk chocolate, streaked with black chocolate, and studded with bits of hazelnut. It will be kept in a deep freeze until it is eaten. Yum, yum.

The client wants you to:

- Give the product a *name*.

- Design a *wrapper* for the product.

- Design the *advertisement* with a picture of the product, some words to help sell the product, and an exciting background.

The written and visual aspects together should make a successful ad.

All that you have to do is to make *rough sketches* of your ideas. At this stage it is the ideas that matter. When you have finished (*in no more than 30 minutes*) the Director will present your ideas to the Client (and to the whole class). The Client will then choose one advertising agency from among all the groups to be responsible for the final advertisement, saying why this ad, their design and name were chosen.

In real life the advertising agency would then suggest a **budget** to design the ad and to buy newspaper space on a particular page and days...

The business of *persuasion* has taken another step forward...

Hint

You might want to decide on the *name* of the product as a whole group, working together. You might then divide – one smaller group working on the wrapper, the other on the newspaper ad. Or you might want to work on everything together. This is for the *Director* to decide.

Talking it over

Gather other advertisements from newspapers and magazines, preferably big enough for the whole class to see. Bring them in, and talk about them in terms of the **description**s of the products. Use some of the **definition**s and **description**s at the end of this section to help your discussion.

Glossary

Description
An account of how something or someone looks.
Definition
An explanation of the meaning of a word or image.

Techniques used in advertising

The following ideas and technical terms describe a few of the **techniques** used in advertisements. You might want to talk about them with your teacher, looking at the print advertisements you have brought in from newspapers and magazines to find examples.

Concepts/skills

- slogans/tags: e.g. *In space no-one can hear you scream* (the tagline for a sci fi/horror movie called **Alien**)

- rule-breaking writing: e.g. *Irn-Bru*

- word play such as repetition, and use of similes, metaphors, alliteration – figurative language: *P-p-p-pick up a Penguin*

- fitting the right words into the overall lay-out of words and pictures.

Visual concepts/skills

- positioning the writing and pictures

- use of colour

- use of lettering (there are many **fonts**)

- choosing the 'right' images (people, places, objects, etc.)

- using the 'right' pictures/drawings/montage and their different effects.

Always remember the purpose of the advertisement, and its target audience.

pages 51-60

Font

You'll see different sorts of type in this book. Each of them is called a font, and all of them have names.

21 Persuasion part three

Book, play and film reviews

> The purpose of this kind of writing in newspapers and magazines is usually to persuade the reader to go to see the film or play, or to read the book – especially if the reviewer likes it! But reviews differ one from another. Some have other, additional purposes...

Your task

Read the two *book reviews* below and **decide** which one would *persuade* you to read the book. In pairs you should say why you were persuaded and write your answers in the format below – copied into your jotter and made bigger to fit your writing.

Topic	What Review A tells me	What Review B tells me
plot		
characters		
why I should read it		

These texts are available for DARTs activities.

Review A

What can I say? **Ghost Dancers of the Deck** is great. Whether you've read the first book lots of times (most of us have) or are new to Peter Slipper and his world, this second book will leave you gasping at the sheer brilliance of it. The plot is exciting and keeps you reading with the many plot twists and the brilliant adventures of Peter Slipper and his friends. The book is simply ace. You must read it!

Review B

Ghost Dancers of the Deck is the second book in what looks like being a long series. It continues where the first left off and is another fantastic adventure combined with fun and plenty of suspense.

Peter Slipper is forced to endure a damp and dreary Christmas with his mother's parents, the repulsive Snavelys, at their Scottish castle. Here he is forced to read the **Boke of Magick**, which he must master, only in the dead of night.

A woman with green hair and a cat has been seen farther down the glen and Peter knows that this must be Mistress Whistles and her familiar, Fiddle. He realises he must flee and manages, after many disastrous efforts - one sets the castle ablaze, another awakens a sleeping monster in the loch - to open a Folding into World Q, the crazy World of Morningland, where he again meets up with Henry Snabbles, the Players, and the creaky old magician, Malahain of Glask. From Malahain he discovers that his parents may yet be alive but locked as Ghost Dancers into the deck of Grimoire cards now in Mistress Whistles' Infinite Baggage.

With his friends the Players, and their never-ending Games, Peter returns to World D (our world) and is instantly confronted by the Knights of Night, searching for the Unsearchable and determined to find it. Peter and the Players entertain them (and us) until the Knights lose their powers in arriving daylight.

And this is not a tenth of the way through a book that will leave you gasping for more. Should Peter learn about magic before trying to rescue his parents? How can he discover the real reasons behind their disappearance? How can he escape from the clutches of Mistress Whistles, and the all-seeing, eyes of Fiddle? Will he ever find World Z, the World of Solutions? The only way you can discover the answers to these questions is to read the book for yourself. You will not be disappointed.

Look a little closer at **Review B** to see how the author has tried to persuade us to read the book.

1 On your photocopied sheet **highlight** or **underline** the different *events* in the **plot** which are outlined in the review. Why do you think the author has used these events?

2 Now **highlight** or **underline** the *words* and *phrases* which the author uses to make us

- feel sorry for Peter
- admire him.

3 **Highlight** or **underline** where the author has used *questions* to make you want to find out the answers.

Writing challenges

Glossary

Purpose
The main intention or reason for doing something.

Write a *book review* of a story **you** have just read. Remember who the **audience** is going to be and that the **purpose** is to *persuade* them to read the book too. These questions should help:

- What kind of opening sentence do you need?

- What words can you choose to make your reader care about what happens to the main character?

- What main events in the plot are you going to tell and which ones are you going to leave for the reader to discover?

- How can you divide your writing up into paragraphs to make it easier for the reader to understand your main points?

- What questions can you ask to make them curious enough that they will read the book in order to find out the answers?

- How are you going to end it?

STOP! Once you have written your review, **swap** it with someone else in the class and ask them how you could make it more persuasive.

Blurbs

Blurbs are short, persuasive book reviews, or summaries, put on to books by publishers to help sell them. *Turnstones 1* has a blurb. Can you find it?

Some pupils decided to make a selection of these blurbs into a database using AppleWorks so that others in the class could search through titles or authors or themes to try to find a book which they would really enjoy. The blurbs they used might give you some more ideas for this style of writing. You might also want to make up a database of your own class's reading suggestions.

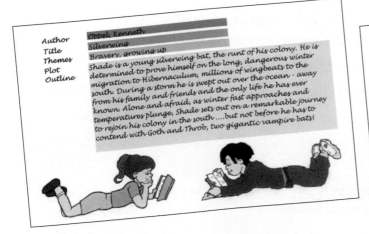

Author: Oppel, Kenneth
Title: Silverwing
Themes: Bravery, growing up
Plot Outline: Shade is a young silverwing bat, the runt of his colony. He is determined to prove himself on the long, dangerous winter migration to Hibernaculum, millions of wingbeats to the south. During a storm he is swept out over the ocean - away from his family and friends and the only life he has ever known. Alone and afraid, as winter fast approaches and temperatures plunge, Shade sets out on a remarkable journey to rejoin his colony in the south ....but not before he has to contend with Goth and Throb, two gigantic vampire bats!

Author: Wilson, Jacqueline
Title: Girls Under Pressure
Themes: Growing up, dieting
Plot Outline: "It's diet time for me: I'm just so horribly, hugely F-A-T! This time I'm sticking to it - no matter what- or they'll be calling me Ellie the Elephant if I'm not careful. My friends Nadine and Magda think I'm mad - but it's alright for them: Nadine looks like a model - and has a chance to be a real cover girl! Magda is drop - dead - gorgeous (though boys always seem to get the wrong idea about her.)" How does Ellie come to terms with how she looks?

Reviewing visual material

How would a review of a film, TV programme or video be different from a book review? What things could you write about to make one of these things sound really interesting.   Special effects, the actors, the set, the script, the costumes, what?

A writing frame

Write a review of a *video*, a *video game*, *TV programme* or *film* you saw recently, and either liked or loathed. Say why.

If you can't think how to start this, you might want to use a **writing frame** to help you to plan out your ideas. Copy one frame into your jotter, leaving lots of space for your writing. *You* might want to write in the same style as one of the book reviews and you might find the structure below is helpful.   You have to decide what to write but remember you are trying to produce a very powerful, *persuasive* piece of writing.

I think that (name of your text) was...

Because...

The reasons for my thinking this are, firstly...

Another reason is...

Moreover,...

because...

Finally, this was an excellent/dreadful (film, videogame, video, TV programme, book etc.)

because

See Teaching Resources

Once you've used this writing frame to get you started, edit and redraft your review as it might appear in a newspaper or magazine. Give your review a title.

Glossary

Redraft
A piece of writing rewritten after editing (also used, as here, as a verb).

22 Debate part one

Talking things over

When people have problems, they often gather together to try to reach solutions to their difficulties by talking together.   This is called debating. Sometimes debating is organised and a topic is put up to be discussed. This is called a formal debate. Debating in this way helps us to think clearly and to have confidence talking in public. This is the kind of debating you're going to practise now.

Glossary

Point of view
A person's, or character's, way of looking at things. An author will often tell a story from a particular character's point of view.

pages 104-107

What is a debate?

A debate involves:

- having something to talk over and about which people usually disagree: *politics*, yes? *paint*, no? But people can easily disagree about most things. Even about paint, especially when it is being put on walls!

- an attempt to make people see another **point of view**, to change their opinions, to **persuade** them that one view is best.

- a conclusion with maybe winners, maybe losers, maybe no change at all in the opinions of the debaters.

If some of you could not agree about the meaning of the word *debate*, or if anyone was not certain, you could have always looked it up in a dictionary, couldn't you? To save time we'll do it for you.

The dictionary says: '**Debate**: *a formal discussion in which opposing arguments are put forward.*'

Glossary

Chair
The person who manages a meeting *and*, when a **verb**, as here, performing *as* a chair.

So, what does *formal* mean? What's a *discussion?* What is meant by *opposing arguments?* And what's involved in putting them *forward?* You could spend your life with your nose in a dictionary!

So let's look at this word *formal* and the other bits of the definition will fall into place. Get into a group and read the next section together and the one that follows, **talking** things over as you do so. If you've debated before and know about formal debates, you should **chair** this group session.

What is a *formal* debate?

Formal is an **adjective** adding ideas of *pattern*, *order*, *ceremony*, and *regularity of form* to **nouns**. Attach *formal* to *dress*, to *gardens*, and to *behaviour* to see what it adds. Work out what they mean together. So a *formal debate* will be discussion with pattern, ceremony, regularity of form – *and* order. If you watch a session of the UK Parliament during a debate you'll sometimes hear the Speaker shout out, 'Order! Order!! Order!!!' more and more loudly, until what happens?

The **diagram** shows you what a formal debate looks like.

> **Glossary**
>
> **Diagram**
> A drawing of something, *and/or* of a process, often showing how they/it work(s).

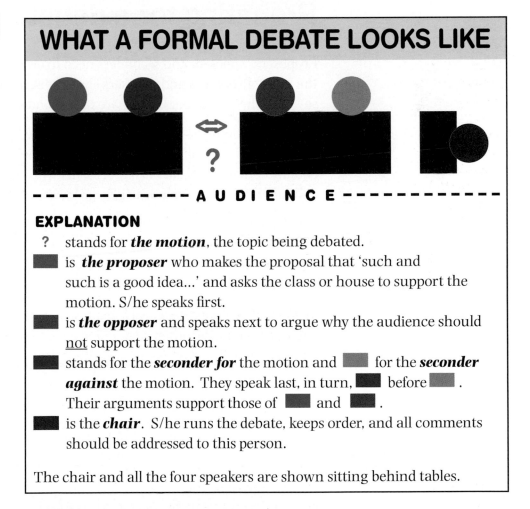

WHAT A FORMAL DEBATE LOOKS LIKE

- - - - - - - - - - - - - - - - A U D I E N C E - - - - - - - - - - - - - -

EXPLANATION

?   stands for ***the motion***, the topic being debated.

   is ***the proposer*** who makes the proposal that 'such and such is a good idea...' and asks the class or house to support the motion. S/he speaks first.

   is ***the opposer*** and speaks next to argue why the audience should <u>not</u> support the motion.

   stands for the ***seconder for*** the motion and   for the ***seconder against*** the motion. They speak last, in turn,   before   . Their arguments support those of   and   .

   is the ***chair***. S/he runs the debate, keeps order, and all comments should be addressed to this person.

The chair and all the four speakers are shown sitting behind tables.

The **proposers** each speak for an equal length of time. The **seconders** then speak for an equal, but lesser, length of time. After this, the **chair** invites speakers from *the floor* – the audience – to express their views.

The proposers then sum up their cases, perhaps dealing with points made from the floor, speaking again for an equal length of time and again in turn, **A** before **B**.

After this, a **vote** is taken, to decide if the motion has been *lost* or *carried* (won).

Talking it over

pages 120-122

We have looked at the pattern of a *formal* debate. You can also have **informal** debates with less rules, and less formal procedures. In groups **decide** what such debates might look like. Which parts and/or rules of a formal debate would it be important to keep? Why?

Do you think that people will change their minds during a formal debate? If they do so is it because one pair of speakers is more convincing than the other? Are there other reasons?

Preparing for a debate

Proposers, opposers and seconders need to do research to find out about the topic. Proposers and opposers should discuss what they are going to say with their seconders. They are *teams*, and should behave like a team.

Everybody should be able to make speeches expressing their views convincingly and the proposers and opposers should be able to answer, equally convincingly, any disagreements with their beliefs. It can be very difficult to answer people who give good reasons for disagreeing with you!

Speak confidently. You are, after all, trying to *convince* people that *your* views are the right ones. Don't be afraid to make jokes. People who laugh together often think together in the same way – or can more easily be made to do so.

Before you begin a debate, each team should try to guess the points that will be raised by the other side.

If you're on the floor – in the audience – listen very carefully to all points of view. When you speak, talk about what you liked in what has been said, what you disliked, and say why. Ask questions that will be difficult to answer.

It is always best to speak from notes rather than reading a speech off a piece of paper. Why do you think this is so?

Which topic or motion?

The class should now choose a topic, a **motion**, for debate. Some of the class will be *for* the motion and others will be *against*, sides need to be taken. It is, therefore, essential to pick something quite controversial, an idea that causes a lot of argument and discussion. There's little point in picking a motion about which everybody agrees.

Here are some sample topics to get you started:

Political – Scotland should become completely independent. Voting should be allowed at the age of sixteen. We need to set up a United States of Europe.

Sport – Boxing should be banned. Fox hunting is good for foxes, good for farmers. Scotland has no place in international competition in any sport because it is second rate.

School matters – There should be no school uniform. We should be free to listen to personal stereos in class. Bullies should be banned from schools. The Scots language should be used in all classes at school. Books are no longer needed because of films and TV. All schoolwork should be done on computers.

Scientific issues – Britain should spend more on space travel, less on nuclear power. Genetically modifying plants and animals will be good for us. Cloning people will destroy society.

Social issues – Vegetarianism is the only decent way to live. All fathers should have six weeks off work when their new baby is born. Young people should have free access to telephone helplines on important issues. Children should be smacked regularly for their own good.

Remember in a formal debate, motions take this form: *This House believes that…* or *This House asserts that…*Try to make your motions a wee bit controversial to get debate moving! For example, *This House believes that children should be smacked regularly for their own good* might be 'better' than saying *This House believes that smacking children is wrong* – which, of course, we believe. Do you?

Now **pick** *your* topic of debate, and **choose** the Proposer, Opposer, and the two Seconders. Give them a week to prepare their speeches. Appoint a Chair.

Everybody has to know the motion. It should, therefore, be written down where all can read it. Why not advertise it – especially if the issue you choose is going to be of great interest to the school as a whole? You could hold the debate after school and invite everybody, including your parents and neighbours, to come and hear it.

Finally…

See Visual Workpoint V4

Formal debates may sound serious but they are really a kind of game. For example, it's *always* a true test of your debating skills if you can speak convincingly *for* the side you don't believe in! Then you have to work really hard at making your speeches sound believable!

23 Debate part two

Debating informally

You can debate or discuss anything as you'll have discovered in Chapter 22. And not all debates need be formal. Informal debates can be a lot of fun, as well as providing an opportunity to practise your debating skills and to continue developing your ability to talk in public with confidence.

How to debate informally

Three ways of doing so

The turkey shoot

If you want to involve more people in making speeches, choose a **spokesperson** from each of a number of groups. Each spokesperson makes a speech *for* or *against* the agreed motion. There should, of course, be an equal number of speakers for and against the motion.

In this way you might have six or eight main speakers, each with equal time. Speakers should be prepared on what to say by group discussion before they make their speeches. They are representing their *own* as well as the *group's* **point of view**.

Give the audience the chance to ask each speaker questions, or to make points, which the speaker will be asked to answer there and then.

As before, take a vote after the speeches and questions, and find out if the motion is carried or not. **STOP!**

The balloon debate

In this sort of debate, well-known personalities must justify their reasons for being kept in the basket of a hot air balloon. The **plot** is that there are too many folk on the balloon and each personality has to present a very good case for remaining on board. People will be ejected. Only one *will* survive.

Your task is to select a character, pretend to be that person, and explain how important they are to society – so important they must stay aboard and survive this journey!

As a class or in groups, **suggest** characters for the trip. You might select from the following, but you could think of others too.

- a famous politician
- a well known writer
- a popular singer or band member
- a teacher
- the family cat
- yourself!

Think of all the reasons why your character is indispensable.

For example, a pop star might not *seem* important, but consider how important it is for everyone to 'chill out' and relax. Does music helps us do this? A politician might have recently made a great speech in Parliament and introduced an important new Act. A teacher would be very important to help other people learn things.

Use your own knowledge of current affairs and history to compile these reasons.

You might enact this debate in different 'rounds'. That is, you might listen to all characters present their case and once they have spoken, the class takes a vote on who is the *first*, *second* and *third* most important, indispensable characters, who get to stay on the balloon. Everybody else gets chucked off. Then the remainder have to speak offering further reasons for their survival. And so on, until only *one* survives.

The life raft debate

Imagine you have been washed overboard or swept out to sea with some friends. You are drifting along on a small raft towards a desert island.

You have with you some possessions, as well as the family pet dog.

You are only able to keep *two* things with you or the raft will sink. So, you will need to make priorities and throw overboard some items.

The things you must decide about are:

- the family dog, Beano, who has been in the family for 10 years
- a radio cassette player which is of the large ghetto-blasting variety
- the complete **Harry Potter** books (first editions)
- a crate of Irn-Bru bottles...

...or, indeed, *anything* you can all agree about!

In groups you must **discuss** the benefits of keeping or throwing overboard these items. You can only keep *two* of them.

Be very careful as you talk about the reasons for keeping certain things.

For example, if someone wants to keep the dog, is it for sentimental or practical reasons? Could he bark or run around an island and find help or food? Gruesomely, would you eat him if food ran short?

Might you keep the books because you could get really bored? If you are rescued, the books will be worth a lot of money. Is that a good reason for keeping these heavy books? And so on.

After discussion, elect one member of your group to present the case to the whole class, explaining your decisions and giving reasons for them. Allow questions from the body of the class.

See Visual Workpoint V20

Finally, take a class vote on which two items must be kept.

24 Writing

About issues

What is an issue? 'An important subject requiring discussion' is how an issue is described in one dictionary. An issue often arises because something has happened, or is happening, that people don't agree with. And when such things happen people feel like writing, as well as talking, about them.

Issues

Issues are everywhere. For example these could all be issues:

- A local Council has closed down the Youth Club and young folk have nowhere to go.

- A family have very noisy neighbours and cannot get the police to do anything about it.

- A pupil has been told not to wear jeans to school and disagrees with the decision.

- It has been suggested that pupils of all ages in schools should carry Identity Cards (relax, this is *not* true!).

An issue is usually quite *controversial* and people do not all have the same views about it. An issue often makes people want to express their views about it to other people.

To tell other people about your feelings on particular issues you might *speak* about them or *write* about them. In the examples above, you might write to the Council about the Youth Club. You might write a letter to the Police in support of the family with noisy neighbours. You might write an article for, or a letter to, a newspaper giving your views on Identity Cards.

But before we can write about an issue we have to think about it very carefully.

Issue one

Here is an extract from a short story about a man who wins the Lottery.

There wes dizzens mair: hameless fowk; double-glazing; auld mithers gaun intae hames; pension plans; disabelt brithers; investment schemes; cancer patients; fittet kitchens; blin fowk needin guide dugs; timeshare flats I Ibiza; alcoholic faithers; credit cairds; giftet bairns; health insurance; fowk wi AIDS; life assurance; drug addiction counselling... There wes letters an aa. *Dear Mr MacLaren, I am writing to tell you about an excellent investment opportunity: our tax-free Gift for Giving Scheme...*

He struggled ti sort them aa out, tae sort the real frae the false, the needy frae the greidy an he gied awa thousans, hunners o thousans, a million, twa million: an the mair he gied awa, the mair fowk neidet, wantet, the mair fowk at sent him letters, cam tae the door. An Maw an Paw stairtet tae fecht, no ower whit ye micht think – like the fowk comin tae the door or telephonin at aa hours – but ower daft stuff, like there bein nae milk at breakfast. It wesna juist a wee argie-bargie nou an again, but real fechtin, staunnin up, roarin at each ither while me an Colin kept our heids doun. Maw wes getting weary, 'I wish we'd never won,' she tellt me.

From **A Personal Jesus** by Dauvit Alexander (A Braw Brew, Watergaw, 1997).

You might consider some of the following issues:

- **Should** people be allowed to win huge sums of money?

- **How much** of a person's winnings should they give to charity?

- **Is it best** to remain anonymous if you win a lot of money?

- **Which people** do you think are the most needy from those listed?

- **What can people do** if they find their lives are changed for the worse by winning money?

- **What would you do** with such a lot of money?

Choose an issue raised here that you would like to write about. Decide who **you** are going to raise this issue with. It might be the Charities Lottery Board or a magazine that has carried a story about lottery earnings, or a problem page in a newspaper. Decide **what** you are going to write: a letter or an article.

Glossary

Conclusion
A final decision **or** the summing up of ideas in, or at the end of, a text.

Letter to a newspaper

Set out your letter in three main sections:

1 Introduction

2 Main points

3 Conclusion

If you eventually choose to write an article about some issue for a newspaper or the school magazine, you might follow the same three section plan. Again, decide which issue you want to raise and who your likely audience of readers will be.

It might begin like this:

> *Dear Editor*, or *Dear Sir*
>
> *I have just read in today's newspaper* (put the date here) *about the man who won a large amount of money in the Lottery.*
>
> **or**
>
> *I don't normally write to the papers but...*

Next, state clearly the points you want to make.

> For example, *I'd like to complain about the size of the prizes awarded in the Lottery. It would be better to give smaller prizes to a larger number of people.*

Lastly, bring your letter to a **conclusion**. You might refer back to a couple of main points, but don't repeat yourself. End your piece with a strong final sentence.

> For example, *I find the way we worship money quite disgusting.*
>
> **or**
>
> *I am sure many other readers will be as concerned as I am and I'd like this whole issue to be exposed in your columns.*

STOP!

Issue two

The next issue we'll look at requires some *class discussion*, *research* and *preparation*.

A visitor to Scotland said, 'The Scots language is dying and it doesn't matter to me if it does'. Do you agree?

If you live in a **Gaelic**-speaking part of Scotland, you might put Gaelic in the place of Scots in the issue.

In groups, discuss this statement. You might want to consider:

- what is meant by 'the Scots/Gaelic language'?
- do you agree that it's dying?
- does it matter if it dies?

See Scotland's languages and Scots for bairns.

Research

To research for this topic you can read books or speak to people or you can just respond in class by talking in groups with other pupils. You might also speak to family and friends outside school. When you are in shops and cafes, listen to folk round about you in your own town. Are they speaking Scots/Gaelic? Talk to them about the issue. Get their views. You might also explore the **Web** or your school or local library for information.

See Resources for Scots.

Compare the Scots/Gaelic spoken by yourself (if you do) and the language of older people you know. How important is the Scots/Gaelic language to you? To them? Do you know? Why not find out? Go and talk to them.

Think of any radio or television programmes that use Scots or Gaelic. Listen to 'On the Ball' on radio or listen to footballers being interviewed. Check some newspapers. Do they use written Scots/Gaelic at all?

Issue three

Here is an extract from a newspaper article about Scottish material in the school curriculum

> The Government has underlined its commitment to increase the emphasis on Scottish subjects and issues in the nation's school curriculum...
>
> Today, more than ever before, there is a huge popular interest in Scottish history, languages, music and dance and there is now good evidence that young people themselves want to explore their inheritance.

Read this statement carefully maybe two or three times. With a partner you might consider the following points (and others of your own devising).

Is it the case, in your view as a Scottish pupil in a Scottish school, that

- 'there is a huge popular interest' in things Scottish?

- Scottish subjects should be taught in the curriculum?

- 'young people want to explore their inheritance'?

Do you think there is an issue to be raised here? With whom? How?

In groups

Discuss the issues raised by this article. Next, decide which issue *you'd* like to write about and from which point of view – seeking more Scottish subjects or seeking less, the future of Scots/Gaelic, our love of money. Again, plan out your writing with:

- an opening line which sets out clearly the issue you intend writing about

- a central section which fully explains your opinion on the issue of teaching Scottish subjects in schools

 - a **conclusion** which sums up the main points you made in the body of the text.

An issues folder

pages 116-119

After writing about these three issues, you could compile an **issues folder**. This would contain the many different viewpoints expressed by everyone in the class. It might be interesting to invite responses from other First Year classes. You could generate a lively debate about several of the issues raised.

Finding other issues

See Visual Workpoints V11 and V13

There are other controversial issues you might consider writing about. To find them, talk to friends, neighbours, your mum and dad. What is bothering them? Read newspapers, pay attention to the news on TV and radio. There are always issues that need to be discussed and written about! They may be far away, or they could be on your doorstep!

25 Formal writing part one

Reporting

Reports try to present **factual** information, information that tries to convey *truthfully* some kind of *reality*. People write many different kinds of reports for all sorts of purposes. Just about everybody will have to write, or read, a report some day. Report writing is formal writing and to do it successfully requires a knowledge of its rules.

First...

Think of as many different kinds of report as you know about. Note *six* down in writing. **Compare** *your* notes with your partner's. How many different report types did you both get?

Match your ideas to the list below. Have you included any of the following?

- newspaper report
- school report
- accident report
- police report
- medical report
- report on a science experiment.

Did you have other reports not listed above? We're sure you did because there are many hundreds of different reports. But *all* reports have some features in common.

So, what is a report?

What kind of job is a report trying to do? **What** is the writer trying to get across to the reader?

Think about other types of writing.

pages 67-84

1 **Story writing** involves the imagination – a writer tries to excite, amuse, terrify, create suspense, and do a whole lot more!

2 **Descriptive writing** aims to create pictures – of people, places, events – and of thoughts, feelings, and ideas too.

pages 85-91

3 **Argumentative writing** tries to create discussion and may help the reader to think things through and to be persuasive. It forces a reader to work out opinions about different subjects and, usually, to share the point of view of the writer.

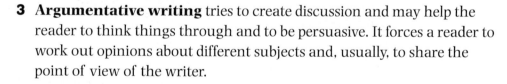

pages 104-107, 116-119

So what does a report do? What is the writer of a report trying to do? What do reports have in common?

You will have realised, bearing in mind the various forms of reporting mentioned at the start, that reporting involves presenting **facts** and **information**.

Report writing doesn't set out to excite us, it doesn't want to amuse us, it certainly doesn't want to make us *feel* anything. It wants to simply **inform** the reader by providing a straightforward outline of facts such as events and actions which have taken place.

Jobs to do

Read the following extracts from a few different reports.

In each case try to work out:

- *where* the report might have come from

- *who* it might have been intended for.

Due to industrial action by janitors and other non-teaching staff, pupils from city schools will be unable to continue their studies next Wednesday. The Director of Education for Glenvale City Council has stressed that this strike action is for one day only and that schools will be open as normal on Thursday. He did warn parents, however, that further action was possible later this month and that they should be prepared for further disruption to their children's schooling unless a settlement is found.

The group was given the task of researching the history of women's fashion. Jane looked at the period from 1900 to 1925; Clare studied the years between 1925 and 1950; Valerie concentrated on 1950 – 1975; Victoria focused on 1975 to the present. Their findings were as follows...

Ernest is normally a very hard-working and diligent pupil, but he does not always realise the importance of completing homework on time. He has a talent for acting, as is obvious in the dramatics he indulges in during some situations in class.

After you have written down ideas in response to the questions, **discuss** *your* findings with your partner and maybe the class. Hopefully, you will all agree. But the second extract might give you cause for disagreement.

Formal reports

Each of the extracts above – however short – shows one important fact about report writing: the writing should be 'proper' and **formal**. This means that the report will *not* contain any examples of **language** which is **informal**, such as:

- **slang word**s

- chatty words (words usually used when people are speaking)

- abbreviations (i.e., e.g., etc.)

- shortened words (like 'can't', 'won't', and so on)

- a **non-standard variety**.

The **formal report** – but not necessarily the kind of report found in a newspaper – will use:

- complete words

- 'proper' language

- complete sentences

- **reported speech** (that is, where actual words are *reported* by someone) not **direct speech** (the actual words said by the person).   For example, *Dr Jones said that in her opinion the building would soon fall down* is the formal report form. *Dr Jones said, 'I believe that this building will soon fall down.'* is the direct speech form, which is what you might find in a newspaper report.

All of this is to do with the **style** and tone of the report. Both of these should be *objective*, *neutral*, *unbiased* and *balanced*. **Talk** about what these important words mean in the class. Maybe use a **dictionary**.

Writing a report

Look at the following information. It comes from *one* source, so it should be quite easy to present in an orderly sequence. Well, it would be *except that* the person who made the notes did not write them down in an organised way.

The notes are for a football report about a girls' match between Glasgow Girls and Edinburgh Girls. The reporter became ill before she could finish and had to go home. You have been told to **sort them out** in 15 minutes because the editor is shouting for copy. There is *no direct speech* so this newspaper report is quite like a **formal report**.

Once you have sorted out the notes into a satisfactory order, **write** the short report that will appear in the newspaper.

NOTES

1   Ed levelled after 48 mins

2   Ed capt sent off 28 mins

3   Played at Scotstoun Stadium

4   April 29th

5   3 valuable pts, now 4 clear

6   Crowd of 500

7   two games left in league race

8   Win for Glas, 4–2

9   Glas 2–0 up after goals in 14 and 17 mins

10 Ed pulled one back after 26 mins

11 Glas keeper conceded penalty after 40 mins; ball struck past post

12 Fantastic equaliser, left-foot free-kick, 30 yards

13 Glas back in front, controversy, penalty in 78 mins

14 Finished game off with o.g. in second minute of stoppage time

15 Will it be a third title in a row?

Compare *your* version with a partner's.

When you've finished check that these changes were made:

- a number of things had to be re-ordered.

- all the shortened English in the notes had to be removed and each word written in full.

The fact that there were notes shows that some preparation and planning for the report was done in the first place.

Writing your own report

When you're writing any kind of report you'll need to:

- **sequence** (or order) your information

- **plan** how you are going to set your report down and the words you are going to use

- **prepare** the report, rewriting it until you are happy with it

- you may also need to use **different sources** of information.

A sample plan

If you were writing a report about what your homework usually involves, your plan might look like this:

- subjects I usually get homework from

- usual time spent on each subject (per week, per day?)

- most difficult subjects to complete the homework for

- **types** of homework: mostly written? involving reading? gathering of ideas/information?

- help I often get (teacher/mum and dad/sister/brother/the **Web**?)/never ask for help?

- the homework I most/least like to do

- other ideas?

This would mean, according to the plan, you would write at least five or six **paragraph**s.

The best **order** of the points might not be exactly as they are above. Is there a more effective one?

Putting it in writing

Pick *one* of the following seven subjects and **compose** *your* own sequenced report about one of them. The subjects are your:

1 radio-listening habits

2 normal school week

3 normal weekend activity

4 main hobby/pastime/leisure activity

5 eating habits(!)

6 *approach* to doing homework

7 preparations for any sporting activity you take part in.

You **must** do the following:

- **prepare** and **plan** the report

- **list** all the ideas you want to include

- use **sub-headings**, if they are helpful

- **order** your information effectively

- write as fully and formally as you can (no abbreviations etc.)

- make sure that all you do is *provide information*

- *don't* give any opinions, feelings, emotional viewpoints, arguments, jokes, etc.

**See Visual Workpoints
V6 and V8**

Remember: this is a piece of writing which only tries to provide **information** for your reader.

26 Formal writing part two

Giving information

A challenge you have to meet is learning **how to give information in writing.** There are, of course, as many ways to do this as there are purposes behind the writing so what follows is about a few kinds only. In learning how to write in this way you'll have problems to solve, thinking to do and difficulties to overcome.

So let's begin by asking questions. Getting answers is your first challenge. Keep notes of what you decide for each of your challenges. **Work** by *yourself* but don't hesitate to look for help – from your teacher or a partner.

Challenge one

Getting the right answers

Here are some questions:

1 **What** are you trying to do with your writing?

In order to do a really good piece of writing you need to think carefully about what you want your reader to *think* or *do* as a result of your writing. Maybe you are trying to give instructions for:

● making something – a model or a pizza

● playing a game

● going somewhere

● operating a piece of equipment, for example, a video recorder.

2 **Who** are you writing for?

Your teacher? Others of the same age? An **audience** you don't know? Do you know *anything* about your audience that might help you to write in a way that's right for them?

3 **What form** is your writing going to take?

Will it be a letter to a TV programme like *Watchdog*? An article for a teenage magazine? A Web page? An e-mail? A leaflet? *What?*

Once you've worked out the answers to these questions, you'll be able to attempt your next writing challenge. What follows will help you to tackle various reading and writing tasks – to help you understand how to give information in a variety of ways for a variety of purposes.

Challenge two

Instructions for making things

One of the best ways to learn to write is to look very carefully at how *real* writers work.

Here is a piece of writing giving **instructions** on how to *make* something. Ask yourself these questions:

- **What** is the writing trying to do? This is the **purpose**.

- **Who** is it written for? This is the **target audience**.

- **How** is it written? Are there any particular ways in which the writing is set out which makes it easy to follow and understand?

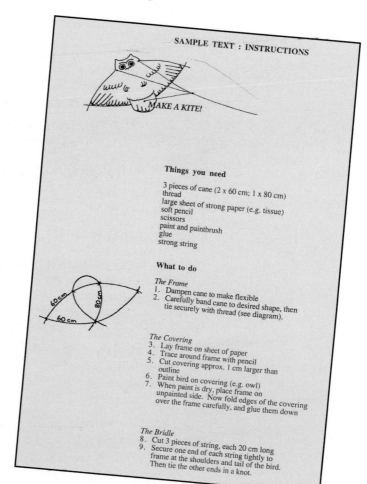

SAMPLE TEXT : INSTRUCTIONS

MAKE A KITE!

Things you need

3 pieces of cane (2 x 60 cm; 1 x 80 cm)
thread
large sheet of strong paper (e.g. tissue)
soft pencil
scissors
paint and paintbrush
glue
strong string

What to do

The Frame
1. Dampen cane to make flexible
2. Carefully bend cane to desired shape, then tie securely with thread (see diagram).

The Covering
3. Lay frame on sheet of paper
4. Trace around frame with pencil
5. Cut covering approx. 1 cm larger than outline
6. Paint bird on covering (e.g. owl)
7. When paint is dry, place frame on unpainted side. Now fold edges of the covering over the frame carefully, and glue them down

The Bridle
8. Cut 3 pieces of string, each 20 cm long
9. Secure one end of each string tightly to frame at the shoulders and tail of the bird. Then tie the other ends in a knot.

60 cm   80 cm   60 cm

STOP!

Pupils in an Australian class looked at the same text. They decided that:

- The **purpose** was to tell someone how to make something.

- The **audience** was probably others of the same age but was definitely others with an interest in making kites.

- They then discussed how the passage had been written and added notes all round it as you can see in the version below.

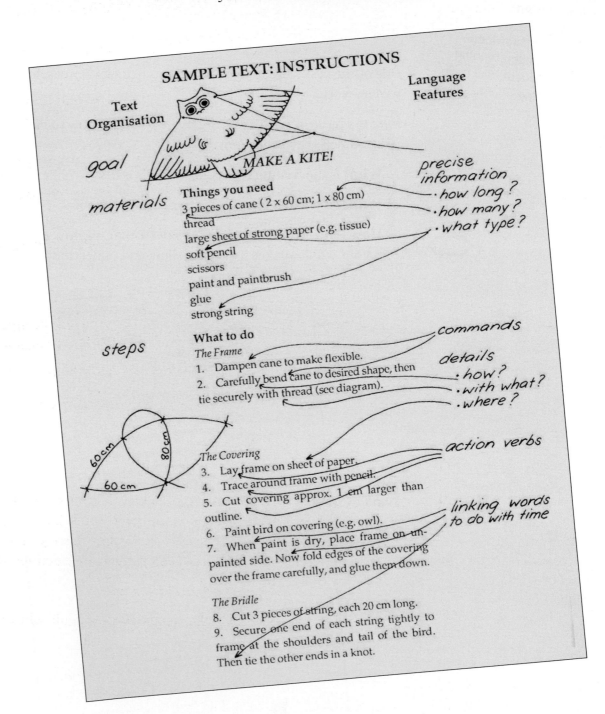

SAMPLE TEXT: INSTRUCTIONS

Text Organisation

Language Features

goal　MAKE A KITE!

materials　**Things you need**
3 pieces of cane (2 x 60 cm; 1 x 80 cm)
thread
large sheet of strong paper (e.g. tissue)
soft pencil
scissors
paint and paintbrush
glue
strong string

precise information
· how long ?
· how many ?
· what type ?

steps

What to do
The Frame
1. Dampen cane to make flexible.
2. Carefully bend cane to desired shape, then tie securely with thread (see diagram).

commands

details
· how?
· with what?
· where ?

60 cm
80 cm
60 cm

The Covering
3. Lay frame on sheet of paper.
4. Trace around frame with pencil.
5. Cut covering approx. 1 cm larger than outline.
6. Paint bird on covering (e.g. owl).
7. When paint is dry, place frame on unpainted side. Now fold edges of the covering over the frame carefully, and glue them down.

action verbs

linking words to do with time

The Bridle
8. Cut 3 pieces of string, each 20 cm long.
9. Secure one end of each string tightly to frame at the shoulders and tail of the bird. Then tie the other ends in a knot.

Did you come up with the same ideas?

The Australian class then set about **writing rules** to help them do this kind of writing. Here are their rules:

GIVING INSTRUCTIONS

1 You have to use simple language or people mightn't understand you.

2 Many texts like this have a list of materials at the beginning.

3 Each step has to follow a certain order.

4 It makes it easier to follow if the steps are numbered.

5 You have to be very exact when giving instructions or things will go wrong.

6 You have to have a lot of detail, because the reader can't see what to do.

7 Diagrams make it easier to follow instructions.

8 It is helpful if you include a diagram or photo of the finished product so that people can picture where they are heading.

9 At certain points you can put in warnings or hints.

Workings things out

Look at the *instructions* on the next page with a partner and try to say if *you* think they are good instructions or not. If you think they are *not* good instructions, how could they be improved? Write down your conclusions and discuss in class. Use the panel about giving instructions to help you.

● How easy are these instructions to follow?

● Look at the panel for giving instructions. How could you improve the instructions?

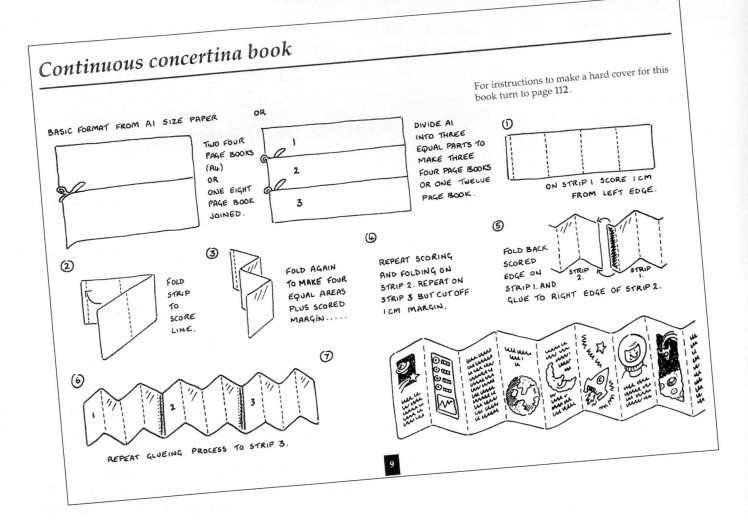

Challenge three

Instructions for doing things

You might have to write other kinds of instructions about how to do things – for example, how to play a game, how to operate an electric oven, or directions on how to travel somewhere.

With a partner **answer** these *two* questions using the poster *or* **discuss** them in class. **Keep notes** of *your* ideas.

1 How would these instructions be different from instructions for *making* something?

2 Would they, in any way, be the same?

Find some examples of these kinds of **instructional texts** and examine them.

Glossary

These are our simple explanations of complicated ideas. **Word**s in red are explained elsewhere in the Glossary. Talk about this Glossary and its explanations with your teacher. Make your own Glossary. You'll find this one on the CD-ROM so print it out and add new words to it with your own explanations as a class glossary. Don't hesitate to change our explanations to help your understanding.

Accent: a distinctive way of pronouncing **word**s often associated with a region, a country, or part of a country, e.g. American accent, Aberdonian accent, etc.

Adverb: a word that tells us more about a **verb** or **adjective**.

Adjective: a word that describes a **noun** or **pronoun**.

Alliteration: using and repeating the same letter or sound in a **phrase** or **sentence**.

Argument: a discussion to support or oppose an idea.

Atmosphere: a feeling or mood.

Audience: the person or persons reading, watching or listening to a **text** (see **target audience**).

Bold: a form of type with darkened lettering used to emphasise **word**s (see **italic**).

Browser: computer program for reading and moving between **text**s on the **Web** (see **search engine**).

Chair: the person who manages a meeting *and*, when a **verb**, performing *as* a chair.

Characters: persons or beings in a **fictiona**l **text** *and/or*, especially as a **singular noun**, their qualities.

Cliché: **word**s or ideas that have become boring through overuse.

Communication: the exchange of **information** and feelings between individuals and groups.

Conclusion: a final decision *or* the summing up of ideas in, or at the end of, a **text**.

Data: pieces of information organised in some way for some purpose.

Definition: an explanation of the meaning of a **word** or **image**.

Description: an account of how something or someone looks.

Diagram: a drawing of something, *and/or* of a process, often showing how it/they work(s).

Dialect: (also called a *variety*) a language obviously different from related languages in its **accent** or **word**s and their use, e.g. Geordie, Doric, standard English, Bajan etc.

Dialogue: the words used by **characters** usually in **scripts** and **fiction** *and* a conversation between people.

Dictionary: a book listing **word**s in alphabetical order, giving their meanings, how they are said and sometimes their histories.

Directions: **information** on how to do something *or* to go somewhere.

Draft: writing (usually) that is still being worked on; also used as a **verb**, e.g. she drafted the report in a few hours.

Editing: the rewriting or reordering of **text**s such as print, audio or visual materials, and their parts, to improve them.

English: the common **language** of the British Isles, spoken here and across the world with many **accents** and in many **dialects**, and descended mainly from the Old English found in southern and central England.

Fiction: a form of made-up story usually based on imaginary events and **characters**.

Figurative language: (also called *figures of speech*) **words** used to describe something by means of, for example, **metaphors** and **similes**.

First person: used where the speaker or writer is referring to her or himself, using **words** like I, me, mine etc. (see **third person**).

Formal: following set rules.

Gaelic: a Celtic language found mainly in Scotland and Ireland.

Image: usually a picture, such as a photograph; also a group of **words** that make a picture in our imaginations.

Informal: relaxed, casual, not following rules (see **formal**).

Information: knowledge transmitted *and/or* received, usually about a particular matter.

Instruction: a piece of **information** providing knowledge *and/or* understanding, usually about how to do something.

Internet: worldwide **information** highway made from inter-connected computer networks.

Introduction: the first or opening part of, for example, a **text**, e.g. a story, a speech, a film.

Italic: a form of type with *lightened* lettering sloping to the right used for emphasis or to show quotation (see **bold**).

Language: the **communication** systems used in speech, writing, visual texts etc.

Lay-out: how **texts**, or parts of texts, are set out on a page or screen.

Mass media: forms of **communication** that reach large numbers of people through e.g. books, newspapers, radio, television, films, music, the **Web** etc.

Metaphor: when one thing is said to be another to help imagine what is being described, e.g. the Moon, a white skull, rose above the horizon (see **figurative language**).

Monologue: one person speaking, usually to an **audience**, in a **narrative** of some kind.

Mood: the **atmosphere** created in a text, e.g. happy, scary, sad.

Motives: the reasons why **characters** behave in certain ways e.g. because they are angry, hurt or frightened.

Narrative: a **text** which tells a story, e.g. a **novel**, an opera, a TV soap opera.

Non-fiction: a **text**, usually written, dealing with facts, real people and events which actually happened (see **fiction**).

Non-standard variety: a form of language which, in Britain, is not **standard English**.

Noun: the **word** used to describe a person, a place, an object, a feeling or quality, or a collection of things.

Novel: a long piece of **fiction** about the lives and experiences of a number of **characters** (see **short story**).

Onomatopoeia: where the sound of a **word** suggests its meaning, e.g. hush, roar, rummle.

Opinion: a person's belief or judgement on some issue.

Paragraph: a group of **sentences** about the same topic, usually part of a longer, written **text**.

Personification: where an object or idea is spoken of as if it had human qualities, e.g. the wind moaned through the trees.

Phrase: a few words which make sense together but do not form a complete **sentence**, e.g. on the table.

Play: a piece of writing intended for performance by actors *and* the performance itself.

Plot: what happens in a story.

Plural: more than one.

Point of view: a person's, or **character's**, way of looking at things.

Pronoun: a word standing in the place of a noun, e.g. I, me, her, him, it etc.

Proof read: to read through a piece of writing, looking for mistakes to be corrected.

Punctuation: marks used in writing to show such things as pauses, **sentences** and how to say **words**, e.g. commas, full stops and exclamation marks.

Purpose: the main intention or reason for doing something.

Relationships: in life how people, and in **fiction** how **characters**, behave with one another.

Redraft: a piece of writing rewritten after **editing**; also used as a **verb** (see **draft**).

Rhyme: usually in poetry, when the last sound of a line (or, more rarely, a sound anywhere in the line) repeats one found earlier.

Rhythm: sound patterns made by emphasising **words** or **syllables** in a **text**.

Scene: a part of a **play** *and*, from this, an episode in e.g. a comic, **short story**, **novel** etc.

Scots: a **language** spoken in Scotland and Northern Ireland, descended mainly from the Northumbrian variety of Old English with, in its northern varieties, Old Norse.

Script: a written **text** usually meant to be performed by actors.

Search engine: program on the **Internet** allowing users to search for files and **information**.

Sentence: a group of **words** begun with a capital letter, ended with a full stop, and usually a complete thought.

Setting: the place, and its conditions, where the **plot** happens in a **narrative text**.

Short story: a **text**, always **fiction**, of perhaps less than 1000 words, usually more (see **novel**).

Simile: **figurative language** in which one thing is said to be *like* or *as* another, e.g. he's *like* a zombie watchin yon telly.

Singular: the term describing one-ness.

Slang: **words** in a special language invented to meet the needs of a group.

Standard English: a **dialect** of **English** written and spoken in a common (i.e. 'standard') form across the British Isles – and elsewhere – but spoken with many **accents**.

Style: the ways a writer or talker uses **language** for a particular effect.

Subject: the person, or topic, at the centre of a **text** or some form of enquiry, or the **word** in a sentence with which the verb agrees.

Syllable: one of the sounds that make a **word** thus in Auchterarder, *auch*, *ter*, *ard* and *er* are all syllables.

Target audience: the particular *audience* at which a *text* is being aimed.

Text: any made thing which conveys **information**, e.g. writing, picture, recorded conversation, sound, etc.

Theme: a main matter with which a **text** is concerned, e.g. love, hatred, youth, age, etc.

Third person: used where the speaker or writer is referring to others e.g. she, her, he, him, it, they, them etc. (see **first person**).

URL: (Uniform Resource Locator) an **Internet** address, e.g. the URL for Turnstones is http://www.turnstones-online.co.uk

Verb: the **word** in a **sentence** that shows movement, action or conditions.

Verse: lines in a poem that form an obvious group on the page.

Voice: sounds produced by the vocal organs *and* how **word**s are uttered in a **text** or life.

Word: the basic unit of language; in writing and sometimes speech, separated from others by spacing.

Web: the World Wide Web, WWW in **URL**s – inter-linked sites on the **Internet**, their **text**s read by means of a **browser** and entered with **URL**s.